THE SPIRIT OF COGNAC

Thomas Laurenceau

Portfolios by
Harry Gruyaert

THE SPIRIT OF COGNAC

RÉMY MARTIN 300 YEARS OF SAVOIR FAIRE

FLAMMARION

1724–1924
Rémy Martin, Winegrowers and Merchants
7

Soil and subsoil — *8*

History — *27*

1925–1965
VSOP Fine Champagne Sets Out to Conquer the World
47

Grapevines — *48*

Wine — *80*

1965–1991
One of the Greats of Cognac
95

Origins — *96*

Distillation — *121*

Since 1991
Time Regained
149

Eau-de-vie — *150*

Cognac — *171*

1724–1924
RÉMY MARTIN, WINEGROWERS AND MERCHANTS

1695 Rémy Martin was born to Denis and Marie Martin on a February day in 1695, near Rouillac in the winegrowing region of Charente in southwestern France. As soon as he was strong enough, he worked in the vineyards alongside his father, harvesting the grapes, gathering up the vine shoots, and learning the delicate art of pruning. He also discovered how to estimate the weight of the vines and support the branches with wooden stakes for maximum exposure to the sun. Unlike growers in the provinces of Aunis and Saintonge, closer to the sea and easy trading opportunities, inland producers such as the Martins did not try to obtain the highest possible yield by allowing their vines to grow unchecked; instead, they preferred to raise and tend them with loving care. Well aware of this, foreign buyers sailed up the river to the port of Cognac to load their ships with cargoes of the finest eaux-de-vie.

Rémy Martin was a strapping fourteen-year-old when the region was hit by the devastating winter of 1709. Frost destroyed years of diligent work in a single season, and the vines shriveled and died one after the other. The Martins' hard-won prosperity almost gave way to poverty, but despite their suffering, the family survived. With the deep-rooted fatalism of his rural upbringing, Rémy accepted the vagaries of nature, and that harsh winter taught him that he should always set a few barrels aside in case of hard times. Eau-de-vie darkens over the years, which makes it all the easier to sell: the liquor acquires both color and flavor in the barrel, becoming less bitter and astringent. Time causes wheat to mildew and fruit to rot, but adds elegance to cognac, which becomes finer and more dynamic with the passage of time. Young Rémy was already beginning to glimpse its magic.

> TIME CAUSES WHEAT TO MILDEW AND FRUIT TO ROT, BUT ADDS ELEGANCE TO COGNAC, WHICH BECOMES FINER AND MORE DYNAMIC WITH THE PASSAGE OF TIME. YOUNG RÉMY WAS ALREADY BEGINNING TO GLIMPSE ITS MAGIC.

Eager to begin his adult life, he was only nineteen in January 1714 when he married Marie Geay, the daughter of a merchant from the nearby hamlet of Lignères. For Rémy Martin, this marriage was also the union of two destinies: his father had taught him the art of winemaking, and his father-in-law, Jean Geay, instilled in him a passion for business. Rémy would successfully combine the two.

SOIL AND SUBSOIL

Cognac: it is a small area and a lot of time, as well as multiple generations of winegrowers, distillers, coopers, and cellar masters, without whom the soil of Charente would never have achieved its fame. The story of cognac is one of a passionate, and at times capricious, relationship between the people and the land, united for the better and—when one tries to gain the upper hand over the other—for the worse. But with every new cycle, the time it takes for the wine to be distilled and the eau-de-vie to age, the two are reconciled.

CHARLES AMABLE HONORÉ

Barentin, Chevalier, Seigneur d'Hardiviliers, les Belles-Ruries & autres Lieux, Conseiller du Roy en ses Conseils, Maître des Requêtes ordinaires de son Hôtel, Intendant de Justice, Police, & Finances en la Généralité de la Rochelle.

VÛ l'Arrêt du Conseil du 5. Juin 1731. portant qu'il ne sera fait à l'avenir aucune nouvelle plantation de vignes dans l'étenduë des Provinces & Généralitez du Royaume; & que celles qui auront été deux ans sans être cultivées, ne pourront être rétablies sans une permission expresse de Sa Majesté, à peine de trois mille livres d'amende : L'Ordonnance de Mr. Bignon du 24. du même mois, portant que ledit Arrêt seroit executé suivant sa forme & teneur dans l'étenduë de la Généralité de la Rochelle : La Requête à Nous presentée par *Remy martin tendante à ce qu'il nous plaise luy permettre de faire replanter en vigne trois pieces de terre dans la paroisse de Rouillac de la contenance de douze journaux*

Et l'avis du Sieur *Rancureau* notre Subdelegué, qui a vérifié le terrain cy-après énoncé *ensemble les ordres du Roy à nous adressés*

Nous AVONS, sous le bon plaisir de Sa Majesté, permis & permettons *audit Remy martin de faire replanter en vigne les deux pieces de terre qui confrontent scavoir la premiere a la vigne de Cuy favreau et a la terre de françois Brian, la seconde a la vigne de gabriel Caillé et a celle de Bernard Sautor, luy faisons defenses de faire aucune plantation de vigne dans la troisieme desdites pieces sous les peines portées par le dit arrest du Conseil du 5 Juin 1731. Enjoignons au sindic de la dite paroisse de Rouillac de tenir la main a l'execution de notre presente ordonnance et de nous Informer des contraventions qui pourront y etre faites a peine de Deux cent livres d'amende*

Fait à la Rochelle le 31.e jour de *Decembre* mil sept cens trente *huit*

Rémy Martin receives an exceptional authorization, called an "Accord Royal," to plant vines in 1738.

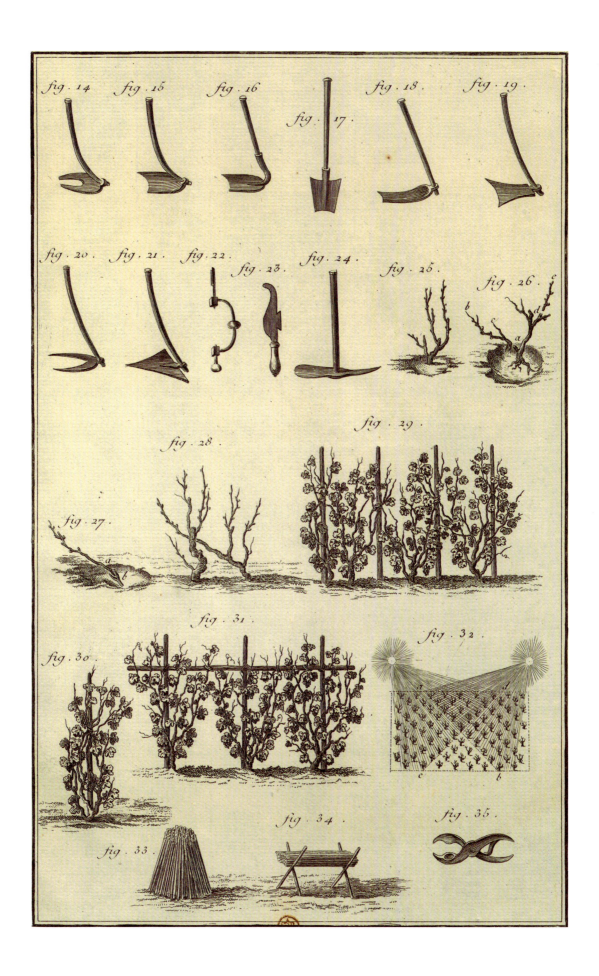

Winegrowing: an illustration from Diderot and d'Alembert's 1759 *Encyclopédie*.

1724

By 1724, the enterprising young man had an iron constitution, a brood of fine children and acquired land, and his ambition knew no bounds. Following the death of Louis XIV, the Cognac region had reestablished its ties with Europe and revived its export trade, stifled by decades of war. The economic climate was favorable, and the time had come to create a full-fledged commercial business. Consequently, the house of Rémy Martin was founded in 1724, discreetly and without ceremony. Winegrowing and trade went well together; as a man of the land, Rémy Martin let time do its work, and as a shrewd trader, he realized that a healthy business had to expand. He understood one of the secrets of success: selling little when a market glut forced prices down, and clearing stocks in times of scarcity. Many winegrowers had to sell their harvest as soon as it was vinified, but Rémy chose to put some of it aside. His cognac earned him extra money, so he could buy more land or lend, at interest, to other growers. Those who could not repay him in cash did so with land.

By the time he moved to the Boisbreteau domain in the early 1730s, Rémy Martin had become a man of influence, managing two estates north of Rouillac, at Lignères and La Gaschère. As owner of land with seigneurial rights, he was already a person of some standing. In 1738, the king's steward willingly granted him an official license to plant two new vineyards, despite the 1731 decree prohibiting any further planting throughout the kingdom to avoid a crisis of overproduction.

> BY 1724, THE ENTERPRISING YOUNG MAN HAD ACQUIRED LAND, AN IRON CONSTITUTION, AND A BROOD OF FINE CHILDREN, AND HIS AMBITION KNEW NO BOUNDS.

Rémy Martin's potstills operated night and day, and his storehouses filled up. On the death of his father-in-law in 1745, he became "Sire" Rémy Martin—a man of the land, but also a landowner in charge of ever-growing estates, stocks of cognac, and wealth. With his many

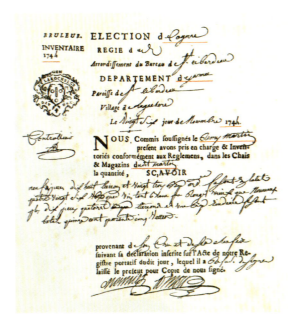

Inventory of the cognac in Rémy Martin's cellars and storerooms in 1744.

SOIL AND SUBSOIL

AN EXCEPTIONAL TERROIR The great secret of cognac lies in its terroir. The soil, subsoil, and climate combine to produce a wine whose depth develops in the pot still. Charente distillation methods can be copied, and eau-de-vie can be left to age slowly in Limousin oak anywhere in the world. But the soil of Charente is unique; it can never be expanded, replicated, and least of all, exported. The process that created this soil began some one hundred million years ago, in the Mesozoic Era, when the various stages of the Late Cretaceous age—Coniacian, Santonian, and Campanian—formed on a hard Jurassic limestone base. A geological event occurred in the early Tertiary Period that profoundly transformed the soil structure of the Charente region.

business contacts and a fistful of IOUs, he bought more and more land and speculated with his cognac.

At the age of sixty-four, Rémy was preparing to stand down when his only son, Pierre, died. Having thought his life's work to be done, he had to summon the strength and will to run the business for almost fifteen more years, through old age and sickness, until his six-year-old grandson Rémy was old enough to take over. He succeeded against all odds, and in 1773, when he died in his seventy-ninth year, his twenty year-old grandson—the second Rémy Martin—inherited a prosperous business. Despite his newfound wealth, the young heir's soul remained steadfastly that of a Charente farmer, and he held fast to his grandfather's conviction that good land management also meant keeping a watchful eye on the changing destiny of his region.

In Paris, Louis XV's grandson ascended the throne of France as Louis XVI, inheriting an exhausted country with a tottering economy. Famine returned and dissent grew, turning to open revolt fifteen years later. Rémy Martin eagerly embraced the French Revolution of 1789. With waves of chaos and disruption sweeping the country, the wealthy farmer saw the doors of power opening to him. He acquired a passion for politics and became one of the most active members of the Rouillac town council. In 1791, when the new council was looking for a tax collector, he applied for and was offered the position, which earned him considerable prestige but little money—a salary of 137 livres, barely the price of a half-barrel of cognac. However, Rémy Martin II could afford it; the steep taxes he paid were a sign of his flourishing business.

1789 The early years of the Revolution had little impact on the economy of the Cognac region. The Charente winegrowers remembered the year 1789 for its bitter winter, when the wine froze in the storehouses, rather than as the first year of the French Revolution. However, the reputation of Angoulême eau-de-vie was already firmly established, sales continued to grow until 1792, and prices rose to truly dizzy heights.

The following year brought disillusionment. The enemy of cognac was neither monarchist nor republican, neither Montagnard nor Girondin: it was economic ruin. The eau-de-vie trade was hard hit by the commercial and monetary crisis, exports fell by two-thirds, and production dropped sharply. A true recovery would not occur until about 1820.

SOIL AND SUBSOIL

The formation of the Pyrenees mountains, about 250 miles (400 kilometers) to the south, brought to the surface a Jurassic terrain in one area, and a rich Cretaceous layer, with soft, spongy permeable chalk, in another. Just as grapevines have particular geological affinities, cognac adheres to a simple principle: variations in the quality of Charente eaux-de vie depend on the hardness of the chalk, and the amount of clay it contains.

Bacchus celebrating the vines,
17th-century engraving by Francis Cleyn.

RÉMY MARTIN, WINEGROWERS AND MERCHANTS

WHATEVER THE INFLUENCE OF THE "IMPERIAL" COMET SEEN IN THE SKY IN MARCH 1811, THAT YEAR'S VINTAGE WOULD BE ONE OF THE GREATEST IN THE HISTORY OF COGNAC, AND RÉMY MARTIN SET ASIDE A LARGE PART OF THIS GIFT FROM THE GODS, WHICH WOULD GO ON TO ACQUIRE EVEN GREATER VALUE.

Others around him were losing their footing, but Rémy Martin forged ahead, sure of his own worth and respectability. Revolution or no Revolution, it was business as usual, and he even had his storehouses enlarged to hold his wines and eaux-de-vie. In Paris, the king was executed, the deputy Jean-Paul Marat was assassinated, and war was declared on England, Holland, and Spain—but the people of Rouillac lived in a world of their own. The locals signed a petition against Rémy Martin, accusing him of the heinous crime of diverting the village water supply to irrigate his land.

1811 That incident did not harm his business or political career, however, and in 1800, the town councilor Rémy Martin swore allegiance to the first French Constitution. His right of inspection into municipal matters was highly beneficial to his own activities. As a member of the town council he was in a particularly favorable position to identify land available for purchase, and opportunities were abundant in the middle of an economic depression. In a period of changing governments, Rémy Martin placed himself firmly on the winning side. His position was now strong enough to survive the First French Empire and the Bourbon Restoration, true wars, and false peace. He had everything a Rouillac merchant could wish for in the early nineteenth century: land, stock, and the power associated with a political role. The year 1811—which would remain in the memories of winegrowers as the year of the Great Comet—brought an exceptional harvest, in terms of both quantity and quality. Whatever the influence of the "Imperial" comet seen in the sky in March 1811, that year's vintage would be one of the greatest in the history of cognac, and Rémy Martin set aside a large part of this gift from the gods, which would go on to acquire even greater value.

In 1811, a comet streamed across the sky. That year, the harvests were exceptional, in terms of both quantity and quality.

SOIL AND SUBSOIL

The 1938 decree delimiting the six production areas or crus of the cognac appellation merely confirmed what the people of Cognac had known for centuries. The best wine is produced in the two Champagne crus, where the clay is least prevalent and the chalk softest.
It's important to remember that in France there are two Champagnes: one, a historical province and wine region in northeast France which gave its name to the sparkling wine known and loved around the world; the other, the one that concerns us and the only one that makes cognac, is located in southwest France, in the departments of Charente and Charente-Maritime, through which flows the river of the same name.

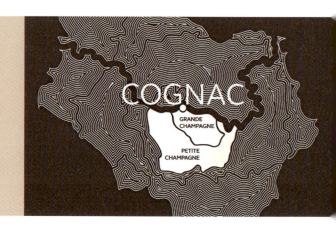

Rémy Martin III (1781–1841).

Advertisement published around 1895 in a Spanish newspaper.

1821 The third Rémy Martin was forty years old when his father died in 1821. He left Cognac to settle with his family in the Château de Lignères, an opulent dwelling flanked by pointed turrets. He was more of a landowner than a winegrower—a rigorous manager, who hid his determination beneath a calm exterior. He added to the impressive amount of real estate accumulated by his ancestors, and consolidated the foundations of an active trade as the sector recovered from 1820 onward. By then, eau-de-vie sales for the region, which had dropped to 20,000 hectoliters in 1810, were in excess of 100,000 hectoliters.

1818 He then had to oversee the inheritance of his estate. Methodical and mindful of the extent of his fortune, he had an inventory drawn up in 1818, at the age of sixty-five. He chose as heir his son Rémy, born in 1781, who was working as a notary in Cognac at that time. The stakes were indeed high: in his will dated June 26, 1818, Rémy Martin II left all the property required for the business to his son. The young Rémy thus inherited not only the Lignères and La Gaschère estates, but also other land around Rouillac, from Aigre to Fleurac, including La Chapelle, Bonneville, and Genac.

> RÉMY MARTIN III PASSED AWAY IN 1841 AND SCARCELY HAD TIME TO LEAVE HIS MARK ON THE COMPANY THAT BORE HIS NAME; TWENTY YEARS IS HARDLY LONG ENOUGH TO PRODUCE A GREAT COGNAC.

Rémy Martin III passed away in 1841 and scarcely had time to leave his mark on the company that bore his name; twenty years is hardly long enough to produce a great cognac. Neither pretentious nor humble, he was simply content to be a link in the family chain. His son, Paul-Émile Rémy Martin, born in 1810, was destined to take over. With another revolution

Those heading south via the sea, seeking sun, first find it there, around La Rochelle. The vegetation itself, with Atlantic pine growing alongside cork oak, shows that the region is hospitable. It's no surprise that the Charente, the northernmost of the warm regions, has throughout its history attracted merchants from Northern Europe, from the Dutch to the English.

Paul-Émile Rémy Martin I (1810–1875).

convulsing the country, Émile Rémy Martin (as he was known in Rouillac) followed in the footsteps of his grandfather, who had experienced the Revolution of 1789. Like his ancestor, he took part in local politics and, in 1848, was elected chairman of the district committee responsible for vetting candidates for the French parliament. Debonair and cultivated, he was also a shrewd merchant. Boosted by the commercial euphoria that marked the reign of Louis Philippe and the Second French Empire, he succeeded in establishing the Rémy Martin brand image, building up stocks, and affirming a company policy based on quality.

AS THE HEIR TO A COMPANY DATING BACK MORE THAN A CENTURY, PAUL-ÉMILE RÉMY MARTIN WISELY AVOIDED THE TEMPTATION OF CONSERVATISM.

A dispute on trade policy had broken out in the region in the early days of Louis Philippe's reign. Innovators questioned the need to continue selling by the barrel and pushed the idea of selling by the bottle and case—a practice already adopted by a number of producers. Traditionalists disdained this new form of trade, scornfully leaving it to merchants newly established in Cognac. As the heir to a company dating back more than a century, Paul-Émile Rémy Martin wisely avoided the temptation of conservatism. At a time when cognac was widely seen as just another eau-de-vie among many, he knew that success hinged on his brand's reputation, and realized that selling in bottles would enable him to protect his products and emphasize their individuality. Selling by the case did not become the general rule in Cognac until the late nineteenth century, when new forms of transport made it possible and the need to combat imitations made it necessary. However, Paul-Émile Rémy Martin did not wait that long; he marketed his first bottles while continuing traditional sales by the barrel.

SOIL AND SUBSOIL

THE LAND OF COGNAC. Cognac is a small town with a population of less than 20,000 people, yet its name is famous throughout the world. The region forms a series of concentric circles around the 32,000 acres (13,000 hectares) of Grande Champagne, which is cognac's *premier cru* with a Campanian subsoil that provides scant but regular water for the vines. Fossilized oysters, from a time when the land was underwater, make the chalk so soft that the roots of the vines can push deep below the surface in search of nutrients.

Different Rémy Martin labels, from a 19th-century register.

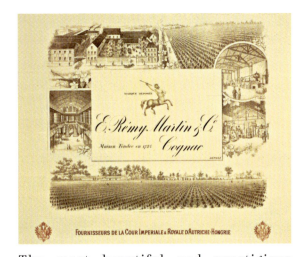

The most beautiful and prestigious Rémy Martin bottle ever produced was the Louis XIII decanter. The ring-shaped glass flask was found by chance in 1850 on the site of the Battle of Jarnac where, three centuries earlier, Catholics and Protestants had clashed in bloody combat. Paul-Émile Rémy Martin immediately saw how he could use this splendid bottle decorated with fleur-de-lys, reflecting the influence of the Italian Renaissance during the reign of Louis XIII. He purchased it and registered the reproduction rights before donating it to the Musée de Cluny museum in Paris. Inspired by this antique piece miraculously recovered from the earth, the decanter was the ideal container for the noblest of the earth's products. From 1874 onward, it was used to hold the oldest cognacs—some of which were made from the exceptional vintage of 1811, which Rémy Martin II had wisely allowed to age. The "Louis XIII" blend of eaux-de-vie sold in these bottles came exclusively from the Grande Champagne vineyards, the superiority of which was now recognized by all.

The region's vineyards were classified by French geologist Henri Coquand in the second half of the nineteenth century. In 1852, Coquand demonstrated the close links between the quality of Cognac wines and the soil in which they were grown. The importance of this analysis was not only scientific, it was also economic. Rectification techniques had been developed for grain and sugar beet alcohol, and the way was open for producers of other liquors to compete with the Cognac merchants. In Coquand's words, "The ease of fraud has encouraged it, and expanded it to such proportions that alarm has spread among the [vineyard] owners facing unfair and unbearable competition, and threatened in their territorial wealth."

> AS COGNAC EVAPORATES DURING ITS LONG AGING PROCESS, IT NATURALLY RELEASES THE "ANGELS' SHARE," *LA PART DES ANGES*.

Accompanied by a wine taster from the Société Vinicole (a syndicate of local winegrowers)— "a man of great skill in his field, but useless outside his specialty, who did not know the

SOIL AND SUBSOIL

The subsoil of Grande Champagne is porous; it therefore retains water that is then returned sparingly to the vines during dry periods. It also means that the vines grow slowly, particularly during the critical period when the grapes are beginning to ripen. In the hands of the distillers, the wine from these grapes yields a subtle eau-de-vie promising depth but one that requires a great deal of time to mature. In the Petite Champagne cru, next in order of merit, the chalk is slightly harder and there is more clay. Very fine eaux-de-vie, aging scarcely more rapidly than those of the *premier cru*, are produced from the 40,000 acres (16,000 hectares) that form a crescent around the Grande Champagne cru.

purpose of his mission"—Henri Coquand traveled the region to compare geological observations against enological data. There was much at stake, with a hectoliter of wine from the Grande Champagne cru selling for 25 francs more than a wine from Petite Champagne, and 30 francs more than one from the Fins Bois cru.

The conclusions of Coquand's research helped to establish the reputation of the great cognacs, but Paul-Émile Rémy Martin aimed higher. If his products were to stand out from the rest, they had to be associated with a symbol linked to the very name of Rémy Martin. While other, more illustrious merchants could flaunt a family crest, he had to create from scratch an emblem that would reflect cognac's richness and ambivalent essence. This called for an image associated with the earth, and with man. An image that was powerful, of course, but also a little magical, perhaps even divine: as cognac evaporates during its long aging process, it naturally releases the "angels' share," *la part des anges*.

The Rémy Martin trademark, from the book *Les Marques de fabrique françaises*, published in 1882.

1870 Paul-Émile Rémy Martin was a keen stargazer in his spare time, so he sought inspiration in the heavens, and turned to his favorite constellation, Sagittarius—his birth sign, a coincidence that had always amused him. Sagittarius is a sign of fire, and therefore of coopers, stills, and liquors. Moreover, the distillation of wine (i.e. the start of the cognac-making process) begins in late November, the first decan of Sagittarius. The symbol of Sagittarius is the centaur, the mythological half-man, half-horse creature. Paul-Émile Rémy Martin thought back to his schooldays and the hours he had spent studying Greek mythology. The centaurs were members of the procession of Bacchus, the god of wine; their hooved feet were firmly on the ground, but their heads were in the clouds. And Chiron, the wisest of them all, friend of man and mentor of Achilles, was the son of Chronos—the son of Time itself. What

SOIL AND SUBSOIL

The best eaux-de-vie come from these two districts, where the layer of soil is so thin that the underlying chalk makes it gray, almost white. All Rémy Martin cognacs are made from wine from these two districts. For a Fine Champagne appellation, at least half of the eaux-de-vie used must come from Grande Champagne. Closing the crescent of Petite Champagne to the northwest, the curiously decalcified soil of Les Borderies cru yields eaux-de-vie that possess a softness that is highly prized for blends.

better symbol for a product that only time can produce? Chiron was also a doctor, reflecting the supposed medicinal qualities of cognac. Everything came together in this single being: man and beast, good and evil, even the ambiguity of alcohol.

WHAT BETTER SYMBOL FOR A PRODUCT THAT ONLY TIME CAN PRODUCE?

One hundred years after England, France was experiencing an industrial revolution. As engineers widened the gulf between man and nature, poets looked to mythology for an antidote. In Paris, the centaur inspired the greatest artists, from Rodin to Leconte de Lisle, Delacroix, and Henri de Régnier; in Rouillac, Paul-Émile Rémy Martin created a centaur of his own.

Born a Sagittarius, he had no idea that, according to the Chinese calendar, he was also born under the sign of the Horse. Nor could he fully appreciate how well he had chosen. A century later, his cognac would be known in China by its centaur alone. The name of Rémy Martin, too difficult for the Chinese to pronounce, would be replaced by an ideogram meaning "man-headed horse." And in the Far East, where the reputation of cognac as an aphrodisiac was hard to shake off, the centaur brand could easily be associated with the verses of nineteenth-century Parnassian poet José María de Heredia:

For a god, cursed be his name!
Has mingled in the fevered blood of my loins,
The stallion's heat with the love that enslaves
a man.

There was no need to look any further. Paul-Émile Rémy Martin decided to make this creature of legend his symbol, barely realizing what a stroke of genius it was. He would

SOIL AND SUBSOIL

Farther out from the center, the reddish-brown soil of the Fins Bois cru produces pleasant, warm-hearted eaux-de-vie, which age relatively quickly, providing most of the cognacs enjoyed by new initiates. Farther out still, the light eaux-de-vie from the Bons Bois cru are perhaps more picturesque than refined, like those from the Bois Ordinaires cru, lying between the main part of the Cognac region and the Atlantic Ocean.

hardly have time to take advantage of it, and only made an initial sketch. But great ideas do not perish, they merely sleep. He later gave the sketch to his son, who finally brought to life the centaur that had first been revealed under the starry sky of Rouillac. From that day on, the destinies of the house of Rémy Martin and the centaur would be inextricably linked.

Meanwhile, the Rouillac town councilor had other matters on his mind. While the Martell and Hennessy families shared the offices of senator, mayor, and deputy mayor in Cognac, the master of Rouillac was Paul-Émile Rémy Martin. According to the Rouillac town archives of 1866, he enjoyed "the esteem of his fellow citizens and the trust of his many customers." A lobbyist ahead of his time, he cleverly combined his political and commercial interests. His offer to the Rouillac council, in 1865, to finance a telegraph cable between Rouillac and Angoulême was not entirely altruistic: the cable would be a boon to his own business communications. Keenly aware of his social responsibility to the community to which he provided a livelihood and which brought him prosperity, he did not forget his charitable duties, supplying books for the school library and selecting his causes and gifts with care, and his fellow citizens were indeed grateful. When, one morning in 1869, a passerby spotted smoke rising from one of the Lignères storehouses, almost the entire population rushed to help put out the fire.

FROM THAT DAY ON, THE DESTINIES OF THE HOUSE OF RÉMY MARTIN AND THE CENTAUR WOULD BE INEXTRICABLY LINKED.

The loss, fortunately covered by insurance, was estimated at 300,000 gold francs. Paul-Émile Rémy Martin was not ungrateful either: a few weeks later, he expressed his thanks to the town and the local fire brigade with the gift of a fire engine, "complete with accessories," according to the town archives.

SOIL AND SUBSOIL

The terroir is also nurtured by the mild and humid Charente climate, with its above-average rainfall spread evenly throughout the year, favorable prevailing winds, and temperate winters and summers. It produces wine in abundant quantities, but with a low alcohol content. The Champagne vineyards are indeed favored, sheltered as they are from the extremes of both maritime and continental climates. Charente's actinic light also stimulates the photosynthetic activity of the grapevines. This light is reflected by the fragments of white chalk plowed up to the surface, literally enveloping each evenly ripening grape.

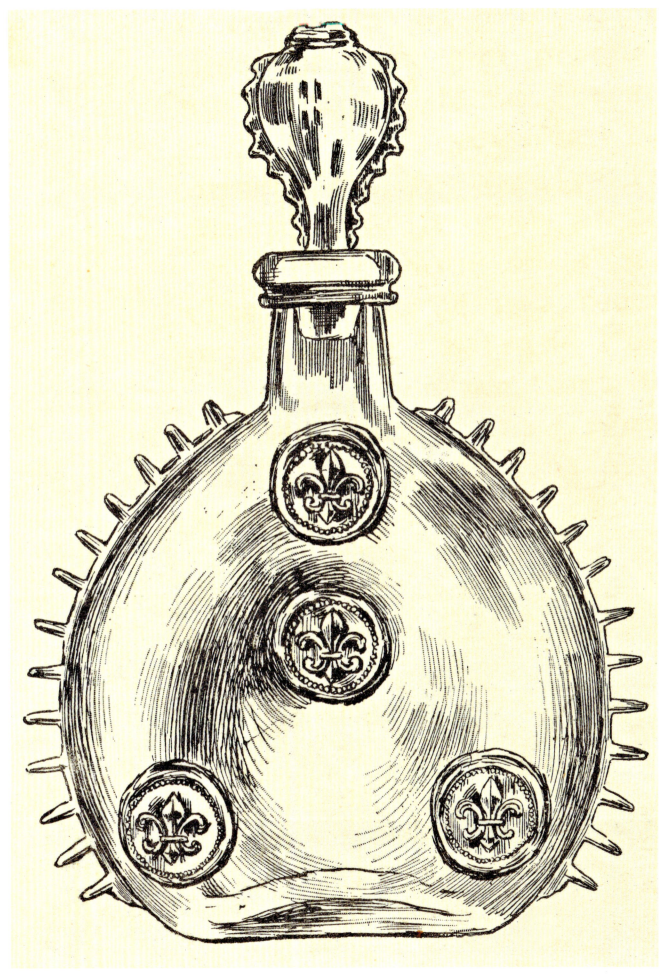

Drawing of the fleur-de-lys bottle, known as
the Louis XIII, from the trademark registration.

The diversity of Rémy Martin decanters in the 1880s.

This was the golden age of cognac and of French wine production in general. In later years, bottles would bear the effigy of Napoleon Bonaparte, but for the moment the region recognized its debt to his nephew Napoleon III. The latter, in power since 1848, was resolutely in favor of free trade, while the name of Bonaparte was still associated with the Continental System, a large-scale embargo against British trade imposed in 1806. The years of protectionism, when the merchants, the prefect or the regional council were forced to take action to defend their interests in the English market, seemed far away. A historic victory was won with the signature of the Cobden–Chevalier Treaty, a Franco-British trade treaty devised by the ministers Richard Cobden and Michel Chevalier in 1860: duties on cognac were adjusted to the same level as those on its long-standing international rival, whiskey. The town of Cognac itself soon felt the benefits of this change. It now boasted around one hundred cognac houses—only seven were listed in 1789—and its population had tripled in less than thirty years. Wine production took off, reaching levels that would not be seen again for another hundred years, with annual figures approaching ten million hectoliters between 1860 and 1875.

1874 Like the other merchants, Paul-Émile Rémy Martin was euphoric. His business was growing beyond his wildest dreams. Trusting his intuition, he laid the foundations for the Rémy Martin brand with the centaur, the Louis XIII decanter, and the very first trademarks, registered in 1874. At the age of sixty-four, approaching the end of his career, he felt certain that he was leaving a fabulous treasure to his son, Paul-Émile Rémy Martin II, who went by the name of Paul Rémy Martin.

In his enthusiasm, he had no inkling of the new threat to the region's economy. Worse than protectionism, the feverish excesses of which were still feared in Cognac, and worse even than war, a tiny aphid from America was already attacking the vines in the south. Grape phylloxera had almost reached the gates of Rouillac.

It would be unfair to blame the winegrowers for failing to prevent the disaster. As there was no effective treatment, they could only wait and hope to be spared. Phylloxera had already reached Chérac, in the Fins Bois vineyards, in 1872, but they had chosen to turn a blind eye. In a remarkably optimistic report of 1874, the sub-prefect of Jonzac declared, "so far, we have not seen phylloxera at all in our region." As if to mock those reassuring words, the aphid was found only a few days later at Archiac, some nine miles (fifteen kilometers) to the north.

FROM ANCIENT TIMES. The vine itself came from the south, brought by the conquering Roman legions of Julius Caesar. At the time, Gaul was covered with forests, with the exception of several drier areas where the Roman established their camps. Such was the case in the Champagne crus, where it was only natural for them to sow their wheat and plant their vines. Historically, cereal crops have never grown well in the area, but vines, which seem to thrive in somewhat inhospitable places, seeking nourishment deep in the ground, had found a perfect home.

The first year, harvests were down by a third or even half. The winegrowers still wanted to believe that this was just a freak occurrence; after all, bad years were not uncommon and were part of country life. Within three years, however, the epidemic had grown to catastrophic proportions and the vines were dying en masse. Production dropped from fourteen million hectoliters in 1875 to less than seven million three years later. By 1880, Charente was a desolate landscape of dead vines. A few had miraculously survived in the rare sandy clay soil that retained humidity and protected them from aphids.

The winegrowers took the landowners down with them in their fall. The latter were forced to sell off their stocks to bring in a little money. At best, they survived by digging into their capital, but for some it meant ruin. "With the vineyard crisis," wrote historian Henri Enjalbert some fifty years later, "ruined owners had to sell their stocks to raise cash; cognac merchants with cash in hand bought up those stocks and blended them with eau-de-vie from neighboring regions. Many of the less firmly established houses went bankrupt, while a few of the great names in cognac prospered, investing their capital in larger and larger cellars."

Paul-Émile Rémy Martin II's initial reaction to the phylloxera crisis was probably youthful indifference. When he took over the company at his father's death in 1875, he was only twenty-two years old and spoke Latin as fluently as the local dialect. Bubbling with life, full of new ideas and plans, he was afraid of nothing—least of all an aphid. But he would soon have to change his tune.

While the epidemic was raging throughout the region, Paul-Émile Rémy Martin II continued to live in the luxury to which he had been accustomed.

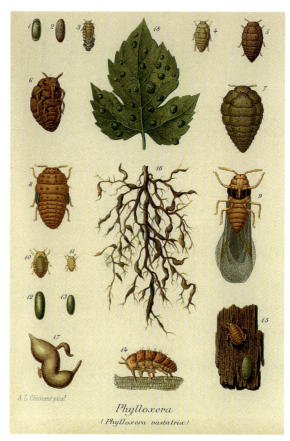

The *Phylloxera vastatrix* impacted an entire generation of winegrowers.

HISTORY

In the third century, Emperor Probus allowed the Gauls to plant their own vineyards, and in the following century, Emperor Constantine converted to the Christian faith. Wine was required for Mass, and this meant each church planted their own vineyard. Over time, the trees were cut down, and the vineyards expanded on land once occupied by forests. These were the three Bois crus. The wines adapted easily enough, but lost some of their character in the process. By encouraging the people of Charente to pan salt from the Atlantic, the Romans also stimulated considerable maritime and river traffic that benefited the vineyards.

Paul-Émile Rémy Martin II (1853-1924).

Working on the vines of the Barbotins estate in Grande Champagne, c. 1900.

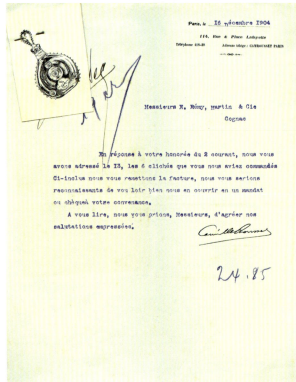
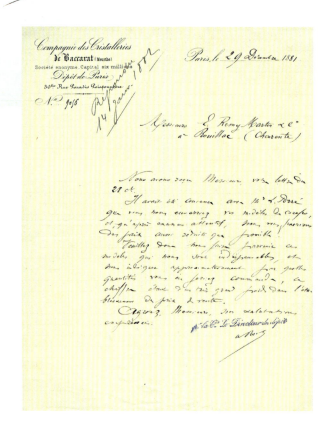

Despite the phylloxera crisis, correspondence was maintained
(with the Printemps department store and the Baccarat crystal glassworks),
notably in preparation for the 1900 Paris Exposition.

He took little interest in the day-to-day running of the business, which he left to his associates, Élie Hériard and Georges Saunier. Heir to a name and to his predecessors' achievements, he was determined to impose his brand image. Like a man planting a tree in a burning forest, he registered trademark after trademark. He began—credit where credit is due—with the Louis XIII decanter. Léon Geistodt, his half-brother from Marie-Cécile Martin's first marriage, registered the decanter shape in the United States of America in 1878. The precious bottle was registered with the Bordeaux patent office in 1880, and in 1894, with the commercial court in Angoulême.

During an unprecedented crisis, such single-mindedness may have sparked sarcasm and incomprehension, but it also testifies to his foresight. Unable to save his vineyards, Paul-Émile Rémy Martin II did his best to strengthen his brand, protecting it from the fraudulent imitations so rife in times of shortage. And as soon as it seemed there might be a chance of replanting the vineyards, he threw himself wholeheartedly into experimenting with new cultivation practices. Throughout the 1880s, he was fascinated by the work of agronomists who had returned from the United States with phylloxera-resistant vine stocks. He experimented on his vines and played an active role on the various committees responsible for rebuilding the vineyards.

Shipping barrels in Rouillac, c. 1900.

> **HEIR TO A NAME AND TO HIS PREDECESSORS' ACHIEVEMENTS, HE WAS DETERMINED TO IMPOSE HIS BRAND IMAGE.**

The expense of all this mattered little to Paul-Émile Rémy Martin II, who was as impervious to financial difficulties as he was receptive to the most foolhardy of projects. The most extravagant of these was the new château he had built in Lignères to replace the old building, badly damaged in the fire of 1869. In this large new château, he could receive his guests with the ceremony they deserved. Indeed, in September 1896, on his way back to Paris from extensive military maneuvers in Charente, the French president Félix Faure stopped by for lunch.

The wine trade, however, was only fully established several centuries later, thanks to William X, Duke of Aquitaine, followed by his daughter Eleanor. When she wed the future king of England, Henry II, in 1152, the Charente wines became English by marriage. They therefore gained favored status on the English market and beyond, to Northern Europe. The port of La Rochelle had a considerable advantage over its neighbor and rival, Bordeaux, with direct access to the Atlantic that could accommodate large trading ships. This allowed the Rochelais wine, named for their port of export, to prevail over the wines of Bordeaux and easily complete with those of Beaune and Champagne.

HISTORY

RÉMY MARTIN, WINEGROWERS AND MERCHANTS

1900 Instead of taking the time to calculate what remained of his wealth, Paul-Émile Rémy Martin II trusted in it blindly, but unfortunately, he had overstepped his limits. His business was weakened by the phylloxera crisis, and the new château plunged him deeply into debt. Any profit was immediately swallowed up by this seemingly bottomless pit. The shortage of cognac left the market open to rival liquors, sweeping away the smaller houses' last hopes. Although weakened and trailing far behind the big names in cognac, the house of Rémy Martin was still standing. The 1901 port records for La Rochelle ranked Rémy Martin forty-first among the cognac houses, with less than half a percent of the market.

Rémy Martin representatives in Egypt.

Paul-Émile Rémy Martin II did not sit idle. The heir with expensive tastes, regarded wryly by those around him, who continued to collect antiques when he barely had clothes to put on his back, held tight to his last mount: the centaur. Unfamiliar with material hardship, he was nonetheless an inspired merchant, convinced that the Rémy Martin brand was his best weapon. He presented it at the courts of Europe, from Germany to Russia, and established it in the United States, Scandinavia, and Australia, where a string of agents worked for him. But this was insufficient; the company's last resources were absorbed by the Château de Lignères, and debts accumulated year by year.

Advertisement from around 1910, in Buenos Aires.

In a last-ditch effort, Paul-Émile Rémy Martin II thought he could sell wine—a commodity much quicker to produce—on the strength of his brand's reputation. He hoped to find a more reliable source of income, and a base from which to make a fresh start. Why not make

HISTORY

The provinces of Aunis, Angoumois, and Saintonge thus began their international shipments under the English flag, until the Dutch acquired a huge fleet of their own. Mariners and merchants to the core, the Dutch gradually replaced the English as masters of the wine trade. The port of La Rochelle was once again French, but above all, open to European trade and welcomed them with open arms, much to the benefit of the regional vineyards.

champagne, for example? In 1906, the clerk of the Angoulême commercial court registered a string of new Rémy Martin products, under names such as "Fleur de vin," "Fleur de raisin," and "Fleur de mousse." Planted too soon in vineyards that still resembled battlefields, the new vines refused to grow. The message was now all too clear: the house of Rémy Martin would live by cognac, or would not live at all.

A few years after Georges Saunier's death, Élie Hériard left the company. Paul-Émile Rémy Martin II found himself desperately alone when his bank demanded repayment of a huge debt. He had to face the bitter truth: to save the company, he needed help—and he needed money.

1910 It was a young man some thirty years his junior who would save the company from bankruptcy. The son and heir to one of the leading families in Gensac-la-Pallue in the Grande Champagne cru, André Renaud had just finished his law studies in Paris. After working for a while as secretary to politician Raymond Poincaré, he could have become a lawyer in the French capital, or just as easily have bought a legal practice in Cognac or Angoulême. But the idea of spending his life behind a desk, drawing up obscure deeds and titles, was anathema to this ambitious young man whose passions were for vineyards, cognac, literature, hunting parties, and horseback riding in his native Champagne province. A doctor of law, perhaps, but a countryman first and foremost.

André Renaud provided what was most urgently required: money. While others considered the investment risky, he did not. He was not a gambler, but he was intuitive and his intelligence told him that, despite its present difficulties, the Rémy Martin brand bore the seeds of success. It would survive by the quality of its products. It would even grow, protected more effectively by the recent decree defining the geographical limits of the cognac appellation.

Haunted by the memory of phylloxera and the fraudulent practices it had spawned, in 1909 the authorities defined the boundaries of the region authorized to produce cognac. André Renaud, who two years earlier had written a thesis on the "false indication of origin,"

André Renaud (1883–1965) a young associate of Paul-Émile Rémy Martin II.

THE WHITE WINE FROM CHARENTE was obtained from three main varieties of grape, each of which had its period of dominance according to the whims of nature. The Colombard, a typical Charente variety, produced a wine that was much appreciated by the Dutch merchants and dominated the vineyards through the seventeenth century. When the vineyards were replanted after the devastating winter of 1709, Charente growers chose to cultivate the Folle Blanche variety, also called Gros Plant in the Nantes region. Colombard was then grown elsewhere, in the Bordeaux vineyards and even in California, as well as in the Côtes de Gascogne region, where it is still a popular variety.

understood better than anyone the importance of the new regulations which he had, directly or indirectly, helped to bring about. The texts did not yet distinguish the different crus of the Cognac region or the Fine Champagne appellation so dear to André Renaud, but they protected the cognac appellation as a whole, and the young man was convinced that, with that legal bulwark, Rémy Martin could rise again. In the future, cognac would be produced from wine grown on less than 250,000 acres (100,000 hectares), rather than the 750,000 acres (300,000 hectares) of the century before, and any fraud could be sanctioned. On March 4, 1910, André Renaud became an associate in the new company, Émile Rémy Martin & Co, with its head office on Rue de la Société-Vinicole in Cognac. The two founders were joined by a third partner, Georges Auboin, a long-standing friend of the Rémy Martin family, and a former director of the house of Claudon.

the only real glory was contained within the barrels. "A happy life is a secluded life," says the French proverb, and this precept was so firmly entrenched in Charente as to be reflected in the very architecture of the buildings. People took shelter behind thick walls, while eaux-de-vie lay hidden in the shadows of the storehouses.

IN HIS VIEW, THE ONLY REAL GLORY WAS CONTAINED WITHIN THE BARRELS.

In the early years, André Renaud took no part in the running of the company. He preferred to pursue his own activities as a winegrower and merchant. He sold his eau-de-vie to Rémy Martin, of course, but also to rival houses. He felt that the time had not yet come to become fully involved in the company; for the moment he was just an associate, not yet the heir apparent.

Paul-Émile Rémy Martin II kept the Château de Lignères, the symbol of his family's glory, in his own name. André Renaud was less enthusiastic about this edifice, too showy for his taste. "A castle doesn't make money," he said; "it swallows it up!" He far preferred the more austere family dwellings in the Grande Champagne district. In his view,

Thesis published in 1907 by André Renaud, a law student at the time.

1914 With the outbreak of the First World War, André Renaud was called up for military service and the company was effectively managed by Georges Auboin. At over sixty years old, Paul-Émile Rémy Martin II was an aging, but stubborn, boss. Having lost all hope of rebuilding his fortune, he was still determined to fight for his name. In 1916, he made an

It was the arrival of the Folle Blanche that led to the birth of cognac. This variety spread so fast as to cause rapid overproduction. It also yielded a more delicate wine, at a time when new markets were developing farther afield and wine had to travel greater distances. Distillation was therefore the only answer, both to deal with the surplus quantities and to stabilize production.

The eaux-de-vie storeroom: marking up the barrels (top).
The packing and shipping storeroom (bottom).

official application to change the family name to Rémy Martin, the name everyone used in Rouillac. The old people simply remembered a Monsieur Rémy Martin, never mind which one. It was as though two centuries of succeeding generations had given birth to a single individual answering to that name. Paul-Émile Rémy Martin II would write it into history—a name he had fought for and faithfully guarded since 1875. After André Renaud's former employer, Raymond Poincaré, became president, he officially confirmed the change of name in 1918.

> IT WAS AS THOUGH TWO CENTURIES OF SUCCEEDING GENERATIONS HAD GIVEN BIRTH TO A SINGLE INDIVIDUAL ANSWERING TO THAT NAME.

1924 As for André Renaud, he was concerned with other matters. Once the war had ended, he was able to return home and marry his cousin, Marie Frapin, daughter of a leading winegrower and merchant from Segonzac in the Grande Champagne vineyard. Business was also improving, making up in a few months the lost ground of the last four years. The Treaty of Versailles not only put an end to the war, but also consecrated the victory of cognac. Germany had been using the term to designate any liquor obtained from wine, but was now obliged to change its laws and restrict the name of cognac to products from the two Charente regions only. A year later, in 1919, the Protection of Appellations of Origin law was promulgated, protecting regional production against imitators.

Paul-Émile Rémy Martin II would not live to see the resurgence of the product to which he had devoted his eventful life, nor that of the Rémy Martin brand and the centaur on which it rode. He died in 1924, two hundred years after the birth of the house of Rémy Martin. But for André Renaud, the time had come to step up.

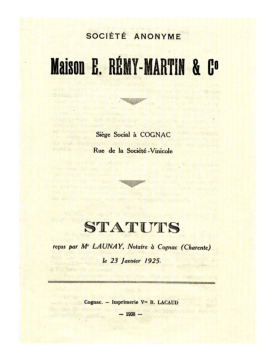

For many years, the success of cognac was linked to that of the Folle Blanche grape, at one time planted on as many as 495,000 acres (200,000 hectares), not all of which were worthy of growing grapevines. Two problems led to the abandonment of this variety. First, it was difficult to graft, and this was the only solution to the phylloxera that had devastated the vineyards in the nineteenth century. And second, it was vulnerable to attacks of gray rot, making the wine unfit for the still. Currently, Folle Blanche vines represent barely 2 percent of a cognac vineyard of less than 20,000 acres (80,000 hectares). It was replaced with the Ugni Blanc variety, which has now achieved almost complete dominance. Easy to graft, sturdy, and cropping heavily, this variety provides a light, acidic Charente wine that is ideal for making delicate, floral eaux-de-vie.

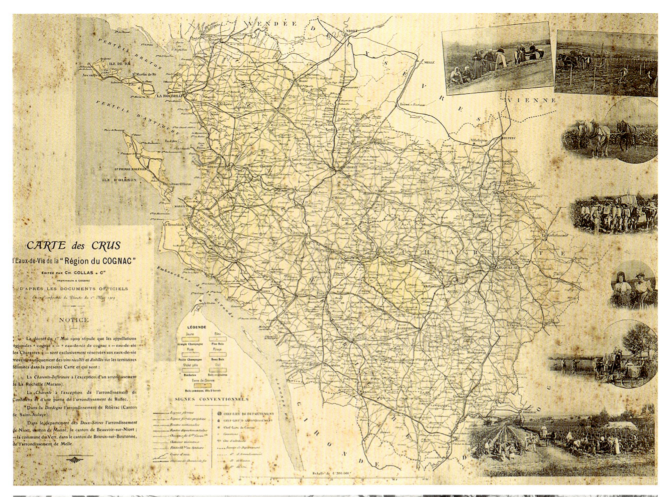

Map of the crus, published in 1910: the "Cognac" appellations are restricted exclusively to eaux-de-vie that came entirely from wine harvested and distilled in the areas defined by this cart (top).
Transporting barrels (bottom).

1925–1965
VSOP FINE CHAMPAGNE SETS OUT TO CONQUER THE WORLD

The business that Paul-Émile Rémy Martin II left behind was neither flourishing nor failing, but was rather lethargic. The efforts deployed by Georges Auboin were barely adequate to keep the centaur alive. After Paul-Émile Rémy Martin II's widow sold her inherited share of the business to André Renaud, the company was newly incorporated in 1925. This marked the discreet dawn of a new era. André Renaud would run the company for the next forty years, completely transforming it in the process. André Renaud led a double life, continuing as a winegrower and merchant on his own behalf, and following his own intuition, the only guidance he truly trusted. He built up his own stock of the best quality eau-de-vie, while gradually preparing Rémy Martin for the future. Gradually indeed, for the venerable house of Rémy Martin would not feel the first transformations due to the change in management until the late 1920s.

1927 The first bottle of what was to become Rémy Martin's flagship product, VSOP Fine Champagne, appeared in 1927. The decision to market a VSOP—Very Superior Old Pale, an eighteenth-century denomination for old cognacs—was in no way an innovation. Rémy Martin had already been selling cognacs of this quality in the late nineteenth century. André Renaud's novel idea was to add another concept: he linked time to the Fine Champagne terroir. Produced from a blend of Grande Champagne (premier cru of Cognac) and Petite Champagne, this is what improves the aging process and imparts the flavor of the eau-de-vie itself. The new head of the house of Rémy Martin was convinced that terroir without aging, or aging without terroir, was useless. VSOP could only live up to the promise of its name if it came from Fine Champagne, and Fine Champagne cognac only acquired its full richness if matured under the right conditions. For André Renaud, there would be no compromise on this obsession for the vineyards of Grande and Petite Champagne, which he believed were the only soils capable of yielding eaux-de-vie worthy of becoming great cognacs.

To his friends, he was a native son of Cognac, an esteemed member of the Renaud and Frapin families, both of which were deeply attached to the land. To his enemies, whose numbers grew as he became increasingly successful, he was a shrewd, calculating businessman, out to extract maximum profit from his Grande Champagne estates.

In 1927, André Renaud decides to market VSOP Fine Champagne.

GRAPEVINES

While the hierarchy of varieties has evolved, cultivation techniques have remained much the same over the years, although a number of changes were made following the phylloxera epidemic. Today, the rows of vines are planted farther apart, allowing room for tractors to pass. The vines are not pruned back as far as they since were, once growers realized that frost is less destructive to plants that are cut eight to twelve inches (twenty to thirty centimeters) high.

André Renaud in 1920.

VSOP FINE CHAMPAGNE SETS OUT TO CONQUER THE WORLD

By the light of a cellar window, agents contemplate
the color of the cognac before tasting it.

André Renaud probably fit both these descriptions. He did indeed love the Grande Champagne area, with its valleys and steeply sloping hillsides. It was his entire life and was the reason he had abandoned his legal profession. But he loved it even more for the wealth he was convinced it would bring him. As the head of a small cognac house, he could not yet compete with the large merchants on equal terms. Only the quality of his products would enable him to rise to the top, and he was convinced that the terroir was the key to quality.

**HE WAS APPLAUDED FOR HIS IRON WILL, AND HIS TALENT FOR SHARING THE SECRETS OF HIS COGNAC TO VISITORS.
HE WAS ALSO ADMIRED FOR HIS RESPECT FOR THE VINES AND FOR THOSE WHO TENDED THEM, AND FOR THE ENERGY WITH WHICH HE DEFENDED THEM.**

Changes in the law proved him right. But had he ever really doubted it? He had even challenged Hennessy regarding the superiority of the Fine Champagne appellation. Once the boundaries of the Cognac region had been clearly defined and the Appellations of Origin law approved, his legal arsenal was further bolstered by the official recognition of the "Acquit Jaune d'Or," a certificate of origin placed on bottles of cognac to certify their authenticity. With the creation of the Institut National des Appellations d'Origine (INAO) in 1935, a national body charged with regulating French agricultural products with Protected Designations of Origin, all that remained to do was to establish the actual boundaries of the production districts. André Renaud would then have won his first victory, and when the Grande Champagne cru ascended the throne, he would be its most faithful knight at arms.

1930 For André Renaud, this recognition of Champagne was inevitable, but before this could happen, the Rémy Martin brand had to be revitalized. There were very few Rémy Martin employees in Cognac, perhaps thirty at most. He had known every one of them for many years, and their parents had worked for either the Renaud or Rémy Martin families in the past. André Renaud, a gruff, paternalistic man who was authoritative but caring, held sway over his little world. Work began at seven in the morning—woe to those who arrived late, for they immediately suffered the wrath of their employer—and ended at seven in the evening, if they were lucky. When business was particularly busy, they were all still hard at work close to midnight. The work week was six days, often seven, with no holidays. Rémy Martin was their life, and it was a hard one. The house was known for its low wages, but also for the deep-seated loyalty of all those who worked there.

Along with hail, frost is what Charente winegrowers fear most. If the vines have started to bud, just a few degrees of frost can destroy an entire harvest. Paradoxically, global warming increases the risk, as the growing period starts earlier and therefore increases the potential damage caused by spring frosts.

GRAPEVINES

André Renaud had a highly personal view of social politics. Paid holidays had not yet become obligatory, and social protections were merely a matter of opinion. Yet if he heard that one of his employees was ill, he made sure that they received a pension. When another was laid low with rheumatism, he sent them to the countryside to recover. At the other end of the spectrum, however, Saturday afternoons were not always free at Rémy Martin. If there was work to do, André Renaud called everyone in without a second thought. No one minded: "We were happy to be there when he needed us," recalled a Rémy Martin employee many years later.

The cognac market prospered up to the early 1930s, although Rémy Martin's market share remained modest. The great cognac houses did not yet regard André Renaud as a threat, but they had begun to hear about him. They accused him of being rude and uncompromising, and disapproved of his habit of treating both the lowly and mighty with the same lack of deference. Nor did his bantering tone and frequently salty language sit well with his fellow merchants. Yet he was applauded for his iron will, and his talent for sharing the secrets of his cognac to visitors. He was also admired for his respect for the vines and for those who tended them, and for the energy with which he defended them.

The young entrepreneur was operating on all fronts, drawing on a network in which personal relationships were his best form of contract, and where deals were negotiated keenly. His policy was deceptively simple: spend less to gain more.

Rémy Martin cognac, ever-present during the legendary soirées at the Bœuf sur le Toit cabaret in Paris.

The only investment he considered worthwhile was eau-de-vie; all others were superfluous and denounced as such.

While André Renaud had a good brand and substantial stocks of cognac, he still lacked a powerful sales network, either in France

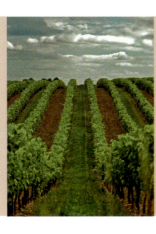

GOOD PRACTICE. Charente winegrowers have always been fairly reluctant to accept technical progress. Chemical treatment is kept to a minimum, and is decreasing every year. To keep the ground clear so that grass does not take nourishment from the vines, synthetic molecules are limited to a maximum, and the *cavaillon*, the local term for the area located under and between the vines, is weeded mechanically.

THE SPIRIT OF COGNAC

Rémy Martin and the French *art de vivre*.

or other countries. He would finally make inroads on the Paris market via Pierre Riviere, an unflagging salesman from the Charente region who had moved to the capital to make his fortune. He was already selling Burgundy and Alsace wines, as well as port, when André Renaud appointed him Rémy Martin's representative in Paris. This was a challenge: Pierre Riviere would have to be particularly persuasive to earn a market share for the brand, which was at that time much less well-known than Hennessy, Martell, and Courvoisier. One by one, however, he won over the great restaurants, which over time became Rémy Martin's best ambassadors with foreign merchants passing through the capital.

Nevertheless, the most important work concerned international trade. Like his competitors, André Renaud traveled a great deal. He had contacts in Germany and Switzerland, but neither the time nor the desire to spend all his time crisscrossing continents. Who, then, would be able to sail the oceans, travel to America and Asia, and find importers to sell a cognac whose reputation was limited to just a few connoisseurs, passed on by word of mouth?

This man was Otto Quien. He came from a Protestant Huguenot family that had fled France after the revocation of the Edict of Nantes. Born in Shanghai to a Dutch father and a German mother, and brought up by an English governess, Otto Quien spoke four languages at an early age.

Otto Quien, Rémy Martin's international spokesman.

This was a piece of good fortune for André Renaud, who read Greek authors in the original text, but had little taste for modern languages. At the time, Otto Quien's father was a wine merchant in Bordeaux. His son worked for him, but the family business had been badly hit by the 1929 economic crisis, and Otto Quien, who had just married, was eager for opportunities to boost his income. Because he was already spending months on end at sea, traveling to sell

GRAPEVINES

But the space between the rows, which used to be carefully weeded, is now often left untouched or planted with varieties that do not compete with the vines. The same holds true for the traditional enemies: parasites, insects, and mildew. To protect the vines from mildew and gray rot, growers have learned to treat plants with a very light touch.

wine, he decided to see if he could find buyers for a few cases of cognac.

> **THE ROAD TO CONQUERING THE WORLD AND PLANTING THE RÉMY MARTIN FLAG WITH ITS CENTAUR THERE WOULD BE A LONG ONE.**

André Renaud was convinced that this globetrotter would be a worthy emissary in international markets, although he began modestly. Otto Quien bought small quantities of Rémy Martin cognac, which he sold in Indonesia and the United States under the Quien brand name. This did no more than cover some of his considerable travel expenses. The first years were a test for both men, but André Renaud intuited that he had found an exceptional salesman that he should retain. Although he didn't talk much, Otto Quien always found the right words to inspire confidence and convince clients. He set up a network of select importers with whom he shared his faith in Rémy Martin—a faith that many in Cognac still regarded as a heresy.

The road to conquering the world and planting the Rémy Martin flag with its centaur there would be a long one. The United States, the main market outside of Europe, would remain closed for several years to come. Shortly after the adoption of the Eighteenth Amendment heralding Prohibition, Rémy Martin, like others in the region, had managed to get a few cases of a supposed medicine named "cognac" into the United States, but authorities were quick to discover the ruse. The only other solution was to ship the eau-de-vie to Toronto, and let Americans finds ways to smuggle the merchandise across the border. In Cognac, the cases were sewn into sacks for easy handling and transport, or even thrown into the sea. This was all very exciting, but hardly good for business. No more than fifty odd cases were sent to Toronto in 1927—a lot of work for nothing.

1933 By the time the American market reopened, Otto Quien was ready. He had met a certain Joseph Reinfeld, a New York barman, who had left his native Austria with fifteen dollars in his pocket in search of the American dream. He was an able bootlegger and had accumulated a substantial nest egg by the time Prohibition ended. He became Rémy Martin's representative for the United States in 1934, and turned out to be one of the most decisive figures in the history of the brand.

Otto Quien and André Renaud understood each other well enough, even though they often had heated arguments. The former spent money to build up his network, for which the

On either side of the treated row, retrieval panels on the spraying machines block the mist from moving through the vineyard, which also protects the soil and requires less use of the fungicide known as the "Bordeaux mixture."

GRAPEVINES

latter reproached him regularly. One day the Dutchman retorted, "I cost you too much? Then pay me commission." Although he had a literary turn of mind, André Renaud could think fast on his feet when he had to. After thinking it over for a moment, he accepted. Otto Quien went away satisfied, but thoughtful. The coming years would be difficult, and if he failed to penetrate the market and establish Rémy Martin in America, he would have lost his gamble. But deep down, Otto Quien believed firmly in his ability.

This time they had established a plan of action. André Renaud would be able to pursue his ambition. He had the stock, the brand, associates in France and abroad, and he was perfectly happy if some people did not yet take him seriously. In the words of Montaigne:

A crate of Rémy Martin was included on Pan Am's maiden transatlantic flight, in a Boeing 707, on october 26, 1958. The vice-president of Renfield Importers, Rémy Martin's longstanding importer in the United States, took delivery of it on arrival in New York.

"The great art of a clever man is not to appear to be so." André Renaud was a master of this deception. He enjoyed this image of a man both miserly and generous, wily but honest. Both a farmer and lord of the manor, he rode through his vineyards on horseback. While quietly building a fortress around the house of Rémy Martin, he continued to expand his empire year after year. André Renaud was an ambitious man indeed, but his dream was more than merely acquiring wealth or even proving that an ugly duckling could turn into a swan. He bet on Rémy Martin when everyone else believed it to be a lost cause. He was about to show his cards, and had a few more up his sleeve if need be. But his true goal lay elsewhere: he wanted the world to discover a great cognac.

GRAPEVINES

Although the winegrowers of Charente inherited traditions that are centuries old, they are nevertheless in tune with the times and are concerned with leaving their children clean air, clean soil, and clean water. Indifferent to the dogmatic arguments raging in the cities, they rely on their atavistic common sense. They know, better than anyone else, that overworking the land will exhaust it, and the best medicine is the one you never use. For them, reviving forgotten practices and exploring new techniques are complementary, not mutually exclusive.

André Renaud in front of crates
ready to be shipped around the world.

The economic slump returned in the 1930s and hit the cognac market hard. The production of eau-de-vie had risen steadily since 1914, but then turned rocky, rocketing upward and then suddenly plummeting down. Between 1934 and 1935, production varied by as much as a factor of twenty. André Renaud kept calm, guided by his instincts, buying when others sold, and selling when his competitors had no choice but to replenish their stocks.

> HE BET ON RÉMY MARTIN WHEN EVERYONE ELSE BELIEVED IT TO BE A LOST CAUSE.

As the world economy faltered and with a devastating war about to break out, the great cognacs were in increasing demand, as if they could drive away the demons of the impending conflict. While workers were enjoying their first holidays, the wealthy upper-classes were living a life of luxury. They wanted great cognacs, and André Renaud could provide them. He sold cognacs dating from harvests prior to the phylloxera crisis, survivors from the Rémy Martin stocks, and those of his own family. Precise dates were lost, so they were labelled "age unknown."

At the same time, he bolstered the prestige of his greatest product, the Louis XIII cognac. Starting in the 1920s, the Louis XIII decanter was manufactured by the famed Baccarat crystal house. Each numbered bottle required more than fifty operations. Each was hand-blown and decorated, a final remnant from an ostentatious period that would disappear forever with the war. This decanter contained the Louis XIII cognac that was served at a royal banquet in the Palace of Versailles in 1938, during a visit to France by the reigning British sovereign, King George VI and Queen Elizabeth.

1939 The Second World War broke out several months later. In Cognac, the young men were mobilized, and women and retirees stepped up to maintain a semblance of activity. Everyone lent a hand with the harvest, distillation, bottling, and shipping. André Renaud abandoned his personal business, devoting himself exclusively to Rémy Martin.

The memory of the phylloxera epidemic and the resulting scarcity was still keen in everyone's mind. For once, the Cognac merchants—including André Renaud—joined forces and limited the quantities placed on the market. Their main concern was to protect their stocks from the German invaders. A luxury product, cognac was profitable because of its rarity. They did not, however, want it to entirely disappear,

GRAPEVINES

On the one hand, they are relearning ancestral gestures for aerating the soil without damaging it; on the other, they are using drones and satellites to pinpoint specific vines that require preventive actions, thus avoiding treatment remedies. Cognac could not exist without the skill of the growers, without their constant research and adaptation to the limitations of nature and history.

A poster from the 1940s.

even if the Paris shop windows had to display dummy bottles and supplies ran short. With sales restricted anyway, André Renaud decided to stop marketing Three Star cognac in France and only sell VSOP Fine Champagne.

A LUXURY PRODUCT, COGNAC WAS PROFITABLE BECAUSE OF ITS RARITY.

Many years later, André Renaud, along with most of the cognac merchants, was criticized for his conciliatory attitude toward the Germans. He had indeed been courteous toward the occupying forces, and even reconnected with an old friend, Gustav Schneider, with whom he had worked for many years. But the head of the house of Rémy Martin knew full well that in such times he should not see his friend Gustav—the same man who had notoriously seized the Quai d'Orsay archives being held at La Charité-sur-Loire a short time before. Nevertheless, Renaud did not renounce his friend.

André Renaud, a keen hunter, did not want his guns to be confiscated by the invader. One day he called Gustav Schneider: "Gustav, you know I have a few old shotguns up at the house. You wouldn't mind helping me get them into the unoccupied zone, would you?" This was certainly not a favor Gustav Schneider wanted to grant.

"But it's dangerous, Monsieur Renaud!" he protested.

"They are only a few old guns, but they mean a lot to me," insisted André Renaud.

"All right," agreed Gustav. "I'll help you get them across."

When the time came to set off for the demarcation line, the "few old guns" had turned into a full dozen superb rifles, along with 4,000 cartridges.

"Off we go then, Gustav!" said André Renaud with his most innocent smile.

The guns were moved safely across the line, and Gustav Schneider escaped with no more than a good fright. As for André Renaud, complicity with the enemy never went any further than this. It was one thing to do small favors for an old friend, but as an active member of the local Resistance, run by the sub-prefect of Cognac, operating under the code-name of François I, he steadfastly refused any collusion with the Germans.

1942 Life went on during the Occupation, and was no doubt easier in Cognac than in many other French towns. In 1942, a tall young man joined the business. Everyone at Rémy Martin already knew André Hériard Dubreuil, for he had just married André Renaud's eldest daughter, Anne-Marie. This courteous young man, whose family in Aigre was also part of

---

GRAPEVINES

Before cognac is distilled and aged, it begins as a wine, and before that, a grape, growing on espalier vines that feed and breathe, grow and mature, that must be protected from disease, but which will ultimately die. A vine that can adapt to many different types of soil, but one that will only achieve greatness in a few specific places. Plant it outside its traditional planting zone—on places that earlier growers had stopped cultivating, like land that is too marshy or at an altitude that is too low—and it will produce grapes for only one year. The following year, the plants will freeze.

André Hériard Dubreuil (1917–2002) with one of the company's international agents.

VSOP FINE CHAMPAGNE SETS OUT TO CONQUER THE WORLD

The timeless pleasure of drinking Rémy Martin, illustrated in an advertisement from the 1940s.

the small world of cognac merchants, made a good impression. More than that, he combined an athlete's physique with a brilliant mind. He had just graduated from the prestigious Polytechnique engineering school in Paris. But no one thought he could get along with André Renaud for very long. He was reserved and his father-in-law turbulent; subdued, whereas André was flamboyant.

Who would have dreamed that André Hériard Dubreuil, the quiet scientist, would forge a congenial relationship with the hot-headed poet who was his father-in-law? Who could have guessed that this young man, reserved to the point of timidity, would one day take over and become a great head of the house of Rémy Martin? Surely no one, save those most intimately concerned. Rémy Martin without André Renaud at its head was unthinkable. In any case, André Hériard Dubreuil soon left the scene, if only temporarily. He headed for Paris where he worked with Pierre Rivière. He finally returned to Cognac in 1944.

Had he not met Anne-Marie, he would have chosen quite another career. Several years earlier, if asked what he planned to do, his immediate answer would have been: "Anything except selling cognac like my father"—or like one of his great uncles, Élie Hériard, who had been an associate of Paul-Émile Rémy Martin II in the late nineteenth century. He was an engineer in the water and forestry sectors, and took a liking to cognac, the product of agriculture pushed to the limits of its magic.

RÉMY MARTIN WITHOUT ANDRÉ RENAUD AT ITS HEAD WAS UNTHINKABLE.

When the war was over, business could begin again in a country where the desire to taste a good cognac rivaled the need for reconstruction. Apart from Georges Auboin, who had died in 1944, the loyal team was still in place, notably with Pierre Rivière and Otto Quien.

André Hériard Dubreuil captivates his audience as he describes how barrels are made.

GRAPEVINES

Even in the Grande and Petite Champagne crus, there are places for vines and places for everything else: alfalfa and fava beans, a poplar or oak grove, fields of wildflowers for bees, hawthorn and elderberry hedges.
These form refuges for insects and birds, which are valuable to growers.
Even in the Grande and Petite Champagne crus, it's important to respect this equilibrium—if not, nature will soon remind you that you've gone too far.

VSOP FINE CHAMPAGNE SETS OUT TO CONQUER THE WORLD

André Renaud and Otto Quien: two strategies for promoting the house of Rémy Martin.

André Hériard Dubreuil then joined Rémy Martin, a house that would one day be his. A prudent diplomat, he let his father-in-law manage the business. He knew he had much to learn from this mercurial but deeply passionate man, but he could already foresee the company's potential.

Rémy Martin was still not a large house. Despite the infusion from André Renaud, stocks had never risen beyond 12,000 hectoliters, and annual sales did not exceed 60,000 cases, still trailing behind the house of Frapin. But Rémy Martin was gradually modernizing, and the cases and casks were no longer carried by horse-drawn wagons, but by two recently acquired trucks.

The export business also recovered. Before the war, André Renaud had created a distribution company based in Geneva, called Arcor, with André Cointreau, the father of his other son-in-law, Max Cointreau. He traveled there often, accompanied by his secretary, Madame Grimard, and Élie Giraud, his chauffeur and confidant. The car was ready by six in the morning, and the boss's instructions were always the same:

"Elie, do what you have to do. I want to be in Geneva by five to two!"

Why five to two? To arrive before the staff, of course. If André Renaud and his son in-law André Hériard Dubreuil had one thing in common, it was an obsessive insistence on punctuality.

> **HE KNEW HE HAD MUCH TO LEARN FROM THIS MERCURIAL BUT DEEPLY PASSIONATE MAN.**

The Swiss business began to expand. At this point, the cognac was delivered in casks, as the Swiss customs calculated duty on the weight of the merchandise. This meant it was cheaper to bottle in Switzerland, thereby avoiding customs on imported glass. André Renaud was incorrigible. Just as he economized by saving bits of string, saying that this was how great fortunes were built, he firmly believed that a franc was a franc—especially a Swiss franc. He often took his infuriating, sometimes amusing passion for small savings to unimaginable extremes: as each truck was weighed when it entered Swiss territory and again when it left, André Renaud quickly devised a way to save a little more money. The truck merely had to arrive at the frontier with an empty tank and leave Switzerland with a full tank for the return trip. The 300 liters of gas meant a savings of 900,000 francs in taxes. This worked until a shrewd customs official had the idea of measuring the level in the tanks with a dipstick.

GRAPEVINES

FROM VINE STOCK TO THE GRAPE. Grapevines and wine must be tended year-round. After each harvest, the vines continue to grow until the leaves fall, around mid-November, when growers return to work in the vineyards. It begins with the first frost—the only frost growers are eager to see. At this point, the sap has descended back into the roots. The vine is in hibernation, and won't bleed when pruned with shears, an operation that generally takes place between December and March.

There were no limits to Rémy Martin's ambition.

VSOP FINE CHAMPAGNE SETS OUT TO CONQUER THE WORLD

1948 His insistence on searching for profit, even small ones, did not stop him from taking major decisions. In 1948, while other merchants were busy trying to win back their prewar markets, André Renaud decided to carve a new path. Encouraged by his son-in-law, he gradually reduced production of Three Star cognac, replacing it with VSOP Fine Champagne. As Three Star represented over 90 percent of the world market, this appeared to be a reckless decision. But André Hériard Dubreuil was a staunch supporter of this move, seeing it as the only way for Rémy Martin to prosper without having to face direct competition from the much larger and more powerful cognac houses. Pierre Rivière also favored this change. Since the end of the war, he had been selling only VSOP Fine Champagne cognac.

André Renaud teaches agents about tasting.

This new policy seemed most risky in the American market. Back in Cognac, Otto Quien agreed with the objections of his agent, Joseph Reinfeld, who feared a sharp drop in sales due to the high price of VSOP Fine Champagne. The discussions were tense, and André Renaud wavered between the opposing views of André Hériard Dubreuil and Otto Quien.

André Hériard Dubreuil had another reason for wanting to establish VSOP on the American market. A twenty-year contract signed with the distributor stipulated that Rémy Martin could not sell its Three Star cognac for more than 8 percent of the cost set by Hennessy and Martell. The simplest way to get around this clause would be to sell a quality superior to Three Star. At the end of a heated debate, Otto Quien laid out a challenge: "I'll drop Three Star in the United States the day Rémy Martin VSOP world sales hit 60,000 cases!"

"Done!" retorted André Hériard Dubreuil immediately.

Sixty thousand cases was the equivalent of Rémy Martin's total sales after the war, for all its cognacs combined. His son-in-law's confidence was convincing, and André Renaud approved the deal. At first glance, it seemed crazy to commit to such a deal, and competitors were quick to deride André Renaud's decision to send only VSOP Fine Champagne and Louis XIII. Some pointed out the storage

---

GRAPEVINES — An experienced pruner recognizes his work from one year to the next, remembering which wood he had cut back to encourage growth the previous year. If the wood is healthy and has matured well, the spur will be maintained; if not, the grower will then try a new approach to best promote growth.

American advertisement from the 1950s showcasing the prestigious Louis XIII decanter and its case.

problems Rémy Martin would face, as VSOP is sold at a greater age than Three Star. Others mocked Rémy Martin's decision to restrict its source of grapes to an area of no more than 75,000 acres (30,000 hectares) of Grande and Petite Champagne vineyards. And they all quoted figures showing that VSOP represented only a tiny share of the total cognac market. But André Renaud ignored their comments. For him, his competitors' sarcasm was just another reason to go ahead with his plans, continuing along the path pioneered for Rémy Martin.

Although he had hesitated before, carefully weighing the pros and cons before embarking on the VSOP Fine Champagne venture, once his decision was made, he never wavered. The determined merchant had taken his stand. To a supplier of eau-de-vie from the Fins Bois vineyard, he stated bluntly:

"I don't want any more Fins Bois. From now on, I'm only taking Grande and Petite Champagne."

Objections now fell on deaf ears. Discussions were over, and the contract was essentially considered to have been renegotiated. All the persuasive skills of the Rémy Martin management were now required to support VSOP Fine Champagne, even within the company. They had only one argument to convince the salesmen who were panicky at the prospect of having to ask for higher prices: with VSOP, Rémy Martin would stand apart from the other brands. The house could truthfully boast that it was the only one exclusively selling Fine Champagne cognacs. André Renaud joined with his colleagues to help overcome resistance from the distributors. The gamble paid off in only two years. To everyone's surprise, Rémy Martin had indeed achieved VSOP world sales of 60,000 cases.

The new VSOP strategy soon proved its commercial value. With it, the diminutive David was able to avoid direct confrontation with the battalion of Goliaths bearing the names of Hennessy, Martell, Courvoisier, and Bisquit. By concentrating on a single segment of the market, Rémy Martin did not pose a threat to the other houses. At the same time, VSOP Fine Champagne was very much a high-end product, and sales matched the predictable changes in the market. Cognac had long since ceased to be a soldier or sailor's tipple and was on the way to becoming a truly prestigious drink.

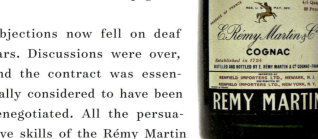

After pruning, the freshly cut shoots remain attached to the frame, and must be removed one by one before retying the vine. The first new buds appear in the spring, growing larger and ultimately producing new shoots. They are carefully staked month by month, so that the grapes receive as much light as possible. The grape starts to form as the shoot grows, first as a flower, a fragile white bloom with a fleeting, delicate scent. The Grande Champagne eaux-de-vie have a magical ability to somehow capture this miraculous moment when the flowering vine releases its fragrance.

During a fashion show in Copenhagen in 1953:
a model poses in a cognac-colored "Rémy Martin" dress.

VSOP FINE CHAMPAGNE SETS OUT TO CONQUER THE WORLD

Calendars inspired by a Chinese legend, which were printed in Hong Kong in the 1950s and distributed in Asia and the United States.

VSOP FINE CHAMPAGNE SETS OUT TO CONQUER THE WORLD

Specialization also brought manufacturing and financial benefits. Production was simplified and bottling costs reduced. After factoring in tax legislation, stocks of older, high-quality eaux-de-vie representing eight years of sales compared with the usual five, ensured financial solidity in their own right.

WITH VSOP, RÉMY MARTIN WOULD STAND APART FROM THE OTHER BRANDS. THE HOUSE COULD TRUTHFULLY BOAST THAT IT WAS THE ONLY ONE EXCLUSIVELY SELLING FINE CHAMPAGNE COGNACS.

The product was therefore adopted, although commercial success, both in France and abroad, had yet to be achieved. Once again, the decisive step was taken with Pierre Rivière. In 1947 his agency was transformed into a company in which Rémy Martin became a shareholder. At the time, few realized the impact of this decision, which set the stage for the vast enterprise that André Hériard Dubreuil would take forty years to achieve, first at his father-in-law's side and later with his children. The new company was the cornerstone of Rémy Martin's distribution network, which was no longer a multitude of independent agents, but comprised a number of subsidiaries anchored firmly to the parent company. Several years later, following the signature of the Treaty of Rome in 1957, other similar companies were created with Max Cointreau and his family in Sarre, in Belgium, and in Germany.

1950 What was possible in Europe, however, was not yet achievable on other continents, where Rémy Martin continued to work with independent distributors. André Hériard Dubreuil, vice-president of the company since 1950, set out to conquer the Japanese market, where his first customers were American soldiers. As for Otto Quien, after opening up the American market, he turned to Asia, expanding his team of international salesmen. During one of his trips, he got in touch with a fellow countryman, a certain Nick Schuman who was working for a British house. They reached an agreement after a lengthy discussion in Dutch. Nick Schuman, described by Nicholas Faith as "a Dutchman straight out of a Conrad novel," would act as distributor for Rémy Martin in Malaysia, where sales of the house of the Centaur had barely exceeded an occasional order for fifty cases.

The first order, in 1953, was for a hundred cases. At the time, VSOP was totally unknown in Malaysia, where Three Star had captured 80 percent of the market. When he began, Nick Schuman had to adjust his prices to match the competition. His first results were

GRAPEVINES

An eau-de-vie possesses a special memory, not shared by man, that indelibly records the entire life of the grape. In the vineyards of Cognac, the grapes are harvested when they reach aromatic maturity—when they fully embody the spirit of the terroir on which they grow—rather than at physiological maturity, which produces the perfect balance between alcohol content and acidity. Here, acidity is not a problem; in fact, it is what growers are looking for, and they may even harvest earlier to adapt to the hotter temperatures that occur between April and October.

disappointing, but he was not discouraged. To his wife's despair, he spent every other night scouring the bars. When he found a customer drinking a competitor's cognac, he gave him a bottle of Rémy Martin. Bar by bar and bottle by bottle, he established VSOP and the name of Rémy Martin. By 1960 he would sell 12,000 cases. He used the same tactic in Singapore. "Don't waste time with the managers—get out with the salesmen," was his maxim. He brought Rémy Martin cognac straight to the places where it was consumed—nightclubs—a remarkable strategy no other brand had thought of.

Rémy Martin's fame gradually conquered the entire world, including Egypt.

> BAR BY BAR AND BOTTLE BY BOTTLE, HE ESTABLISHED VSOP AND THE NAME OF RÉMY MARTIN.

"Luck? It wasn't luck. Our competitors were slow to understand that the VSOP trend was irreversible," he later declared. Rémy Martin was not content just to lead the VSOP market; they set out to expand it. At the end of the 1950s, no one could have foreseen that the superior products would one day account for more than half of the world's cognac market. By the time other merchants realized what was happening, it was too late. When they finally joined the VSOP battle they were, in fact, promoting Rémy Martin, a name now synonymous with the product category.

Throughout these years, Rémy Martin was steadily gaining prestige around the world, in the United States, Australia, Japan, and Hong Kong, where it was spectacularly successful. Back in Cognac, life continued as if nothing had changed, following the pace set by André Renaud and his shifting moods. The Cognac staff feared his slightest comment, breathing more easily when he was in Geneva or Paris. But they were never truly relaxed, and always expected the worst. They saw him at work, scrutinizing the company telephone bills before upbraiding an unfortunate employee:

"You talked to Bordeaux for ten minutes the other day. Can't you deal with a call faster than that?"

GRAPEVINES

In the late 1970s, grapes were harvested during the first two weeks of October. Now, harvests usually take place from September 10 to 20. In 2011, some growers even started picking their grapes on August 31. Proof of the vines' resilience is that they are adapting as much as possible to the impact of climate change.

Delivering barrels to the famous restaurant
Drouant in Paris, in 1957.

VSOP FINE CHAMPAGNE SETS OUT TO CONQUER THE WORLD

Rémy Martin around the world: from Havana, to Australia, via Jersey, Hong Kong, Singapore, and Casablanca.

The employee frantically searched his memory for the one order among the dozens he had dealt with over the previous few weeks that had incurred his employer's wrath. He finally remembered: "But it was an order for 500 cases, Monsieur Renaud."

"Well, if it was that complicated, you only had to write a letter, you fool!"

He even went so far as to post a notice in the Cognac offices, threatening to reduce year-end bonuses if the lights were still left on after eight in the morning. He also put up a sign over the pay office window that read: "Never lend money to your best friend. The day he's due to pay you back is the day he'll become your worst enemy." After reading these words, very few employees dared to ask for an advance on their wages. He clearly struck fear into the hearts of many. When his massive figure, topped by his ever-present hat, appeared, silence reigned and everyone went frantically to work. He had a hot temper and a loud mouth, but was also a hard worker. Whether you were Cellar Master or just an ordinary employee, he would ask for your opinion when he wanted it. On occasion, he would even stop to discuss his vision of the world or share his thoughts on literature or trade. He never missed a marriage or a baptism, always choosing his gifts with care. For one, a pair of shoes; for another, a set of Beethoven records.

He detested being approached with personal problems, but was known to keep an observant eye—like the morning when he found one of his workers looking sad.

Having listened to his tale of woe, André Renaud asked him: "But why didn't you speak to me about this before?"

"Oh, Monsieur Renaud, I knew you would notice one day," was the reply.

> **WHEN HIS MASSIVE FIGURE, TOPPED BY HIS EVER-PRESENT HAT, APPEARED, SILENCE REIGNED AND EVERYONE WENT FRANTICALLY TO WORK.**

This was the flip side to André Renaud, which by nature he always wanted to keep hidden. He was said to be miserly, and he never denied it, but many people knew just how generous he could be. He did not believe in displaying his generosity; this would have betrayed his personal definition of this virtue. In the same way, he was considered intransigent and obstinate, but those close to him knew from experience that he could be caring and considerate when need be.

GRAPEVINES

Despite everything, the vines seek to preserve the immutable timeframe imposed by nature— the one hundred days between flowering and harvest, the forty days from the onset of ripening to harvesting. Yet the vines suffer. The flip side of this effort is that they have less time to rest; the winters are milder and they start to grow earlier in the spring. Year after year, however, they continue to produce abundantly.

André Renaud liked power. He liked to run everything, but what he liked best was his own little world. If he commented to an employee about their work with the words, "that's good," they could consider this to be the most superlative of compliments. His bad temper was often forgiven, because he vented it not only on people beneath him, but also had a field day berating more distinguished figures. One day, for example, the director of the Banque de France arrived late for a luncheon in Cognac.

"I forgot our appointment," mumbled the banker, by way of explanation.
"Punctuality is a virtue," replied André Renaud coldly.
A young employee at the table tried to brush over the incident, giving up his place to the latecomer.
"You, you stay put!" thundered André Renaud, adding sarcastically to the banker, and pointing to the end of the table, "Sit down there—and you can start with the same course as the rest of us."

An invitation to one of André Renaud's luncheons was highly prized. The man who refused the pomp of a great mansion received his guests each day on the dot of midday in his little house on the Rue d'Oran, near his storehouses. His dining room was small and could seat no more than ten. But it was a great honor to receive an invitation, a privilege he accorded not only to local men of distinction, to his friend the Russian ambassador Vladimir Vinogradov, or to the writer Louise de Vilmorin, but also to his employees.

Cognac was not the only subject of conversation at table. The priest and the minister were often there, and André Renaud loved to hear them arguing over thorny questions of doctrine. The fearsome merchant was also a man of culture, who liked to discuss literature and metaphysics while savoring the dishes prepared by his cook, known as much for her bad temper as her cordon bleu skills.

Daily life seemed easy when contemplated from the dining room. Outside, however, the cognac market was undergoing a massive expansion, and Rémy Martin was battling inch by inch to conquer the world with its VSOP Fine Champagne. Between 1947 and 1954, total cognac production rose from thirty to forty million bottles. In the following years it doubled again, then tripled. Rémy Martin sales grew much faster than the market, and from counting in tens of thousands of cases, it then had to starting thinking in terms of hundreds of thousands. By the end of the 1950s, the house of Rémy Martin employed 150 people, double the number of ten years earlier.

FROM THE HARVEST TO THE WINE. Where mechanized harvesting methods are used, the equipment must be adjusted with great care, because grapes with the degree of ripeness required in Charente do not detach easily. The vine must be treated gently and leaves must not be torn off in the process, as they would spoil the harvest. Harvesting by hand is more time-consuming, but is still practiced in a number of Charente vineyards, notably with younger vines—although qualified labor is increasingly hard to find.

André Renaud with his guests at the Grollet Estate.

VSOP FINE CHAMPAGNE SETS OUT TO CONQUER THE WORLD

The harvest 1961, immortalized by Robert Doisneau.

1960

The company required a completely new approach. The time for daring ruses, however skillful they had been, was over. The need for strategic thinking and marketing had become imperative. At the age of eighty, André Renaud found it difficult to adapt. A new era was beginning, one to which he no longer belonged. Age had made him cautious, even conservative in his outlook, and given his autocratic character, he could not delegate even the smallest share of his power. His business structure was still based on a handful of friends. His "ambassadors" in other countries included the Marquis de Vargas in Spain, Baron Sagna in Italy, and Count Cardelli Rinaldini in the Vatican. But these names, illustrious as they were, did not a business strategy make. André Renaud was still reluctant to invest his profits in anything other than eau-de-vie. The very idea of having to spend money on advertising shocked him to the core. Who needed publicity anyway, when Rémy Martin had the best of all products?

> **THE TIME FOR DARING RUSES, HOWEVER SKILLFUL THEY HAD BEEN, WAS OVER. THE NEED FOR STRATEGIC THINKING AND MARKETING HAD BECOME IMPERATIVE.**

In Cognac, the house of Rémy Martin pursued its quiet, steady pace. Every year in October, all other work was stopped while everyone helped with the harvest. The orders had to wait. André Hériard Dubreuil, still in the shadow of his father-in-law, was quietly laying the ground-

Advertisement designed by Jean Colin, a famous poster artist.

work for his great enterprise. He knew they would soon have to increase production capacity, and launch a real promotional policy for the brand name. Meanwhile, however, he bided his time, restricting himself to a number of discreet moves. André Renaud approved them, as

While the alembic, or copper pot still, reveals the wine's qualities, the depth of a cognac already exists in this acidic wine, which is so difficult to produce. And while there are finer wines than those of Charente, none are better for distilling. Champagne wine embodies the distinct characteristics of the Champagne crus, provided they are preserved during the vinification process. In the Juillac-le-Coq facilities, where the entire Rémy Martin harvest is vinified and distilled, everything is designed to treat the grapes royally. They arrive in trucks with air suspension and are then transported along a gentle slope, via the force of gravity alone.

they had the immense virtue of costing very little. He prepared for the change of course slowly but surely, preparing files collating all the sales data they possessed, customer by customer, market by market. Innocuous though it may have seemed, this move was part of a radical switch in sales policy. Accounts would no longer be structured horizontally, department by department, but vertically, market by market.

While the supermarket trade had expanded in Europe, and with the reputation of cognac extending far beyond the small circle of initiates and established at all levels of society, the era of big business had clearly replaced that of the small trader. An obvious sign of change was the marked interest of large food corporations in the cognac houses. Courvoisier, for example, was bought by a Canadian company in the early 1960s. There were two possible paths moving forward. Rémy Martin could adopt an aggressive sales strategy, aiming to increase consumption considerably, or it could instead focus on maintaining the unique character of its product. André Renaud and his son-in-law had long since chosen the latter of these options, convinced that it was the only way to preserve the originality of cognac, and prevent it from descending to the level of an ordinary brandy, like the others.

1965

André Renaud devoted his entire life to cognac. His health was failing, but he persisted.

His doctor had prescribed bed rest, but when one of his daughters came to visit him in his room, André Renaud was not there. He had returned to the only place where he felt completely at home, his cellars. They remained his refuge right through the summer of 1965, when his journey came to an end. That day marked the end of a man who was devoted to cognac like few others, who hid his sensitivity under the thick skin of a wily farmer, who protected himself from the petty-mindedness of the business world by always being shrewder than his adversaries, who always loved cognac

In Juillac-le-Coq and elsewhere, the pressing process takes place in a press with a fine-mesh strainer, to prevent the pips from adding unwanted tannin and so that the juice remains clear. It is then left to ferment for just under a week.

The artist Clara Quien revived the Centaur.
In 1962, she created the sculpture that would become
Rémy Martin's new logo. It quickly spread around the world,
as illustrated by this Hong Kong advertisement from 1964 (left).

and was able to get the entire world to love it as well. The man took a few secrets with him, but left behind his life's work. To his daughters Anne-Marie Hériard Dubreuil and Geneviève Cointreau, he bequeathed the capital of a powerful company with considerable stocks that was selling 300,000 cases of cognac annually. Rémy Martin had not been satisfied with achieving 5 percent of the world's cognac sales.

> **THAT DAY MARKED THE END OF A MAN WHO WAS DEVOTED TO COGNAC LIKE FEW OTHERS, WHO ALWAYS LOVED COGNAC AND WAS ABLE TO GET THE ENTIRE WORLD TO LOVE IT AS WELL.**

The kiss of the grape picker, by Robert Doisneau (1961).

André Renaud made the company the unquestioned leader in the market for a superior product, holding a dominant position in the two finest vineyard districts of the region. Although its commercial dimension did not rival that of its competitors, Rémy Martin had become a financial powerhouse, on an equal footing with the most famous cognac houses. And it would need to be. By this point, the three big names in cognac had finally realized the scope of the threat. A fourth brand, for many years considered to be insignificant, had set its sights on claiming its share of the cognac business. To them, it seemed like Rémy Martin had to be stopped, at any price, from becoming one of the great names in cognac.

André Renaud in the middle of a tasting session, in front of his office windows, Rue de la Société-Vinicole in Cognac.

In Cognac, the concept of yield is different than in other wine regions. A low initial alcohol content is here considered an advantage, not a fault, as the aroma will be richer for it. The wine has an alcohol content of just 7 degrees alcohol, the minimum required for the appellation, and it takes 10 liters to make 1 liter of eau-de-vie of 70 degrees alcohol. Additives are not allowed for this wine, making it extremely fragile. It must therefore be distilled rapidly, between November and the end of March following the harvest.

André Renaud and Louise de Vilmorin in the vineyards in 1961, by Robert Doisneau. She was so inspired that she wrote lovely texts and poems about cognac and its region.

1965–1991
ONE OF THE GREATS OF COGNAC

1965 It all began in the relatively cordial atmosphere of the union of cognac exporters. The uninitiated would have detected nothing more than a friendly difference of opinion among experts. That morning the debate was on competition between cognac and whisky, and André Hériard Dubreuil was defending a view not shared by most of the other merchants.

"We cannot offer a product that is more expensive than whisky," they said. "We would lose our share of the market overnight."

"On the contrary," insisted André Hériard Dubreuil, "cognac is a luxury product and must be priced higher than whisky. If we don't do this, we'll be selling virtually nothing in just a few years. Even if we drop our margins, and even if we lower the quality of our products to alarming levels, we will still lose. A hectoliter of wine will always cost more than a hundredweight of barley! Our only chance lies in the quality of our products—and quality comes at a price."

Make no mistake, behind these polite discussions, the future of cognac was hanging in the balance. André Hériard Dubreuil realized what was at stake after he had been appointed CEO of Rémy Martin in 1965. He was ready to stand by his principles, whatever the cost. He would never challenge André Renaud's policy that demanded quality, nor would he betray VSOP and Fine Champagne. As opposed to the idea that the price of wine should be subordinate to that of cognac, he knew that excellent wines—for which he was prepared to pay—were needed to produce excellent cognacs. If others wanted to sell at lower prices and ruin the reputation of cognac, he would do everything in his power to stop them.

HE WOULD NEVER CHALLENGE ANDRÉ RENAUD'S POLICY THAT DEMANDED QUALITY, NOR WOULD HE BETRAY VSOP AND FINE CHAMPAGNE.

The debate soon grew acrimonious. Should they let the market collapse or should they support it? The thousands of growers in the region were all threatened, as they watched wine prices tumble year after year, sometimes dropping to completely untenable levels. The merchants, however, agreed that wine prices needed to come down still further.

"Annual eau-de-vie production exceeds sales," they argued. "Therefore we have overproduction."

Like the good mathematician that he was, André Hériard Dubreuil did not trust simplistic calculations.

ORIGINS

The Dutch deserve credit for the distillation of cognac. After they became leaders in the wine trade, they scooped up wines from both the Aquitaine and La Rochelle regions. Unfortunately, however, the La Rochelle wines were fragile and did not travel well. As the trade continued to grow, the volume of the barrels became a cumbersome problem.

"You're wrong!" he snapped. "Wine distilled today will only be sold four years from now—at the earliest. The market is growing by 4 to 5 percent each year, and we are more likely to find ourselves with a shortage. By then it will be too late to buy the supplies we need. If we discourage the winegrowers today, we won't be able to meet demand tomorrow."

Merchants had been setting their own prices in the Cognac region since the late nineteenth century. This lopsided situation, once accepted by growers facing bankruptcy, had become unsustainable. The phylloxera epidemic was seventy years in the past. Agriculture itself had undergone radical changes and it was high time to turn the page and leave the past behind. For André Hériard Dubreuil, the expansion of the cognac business could no longer be forced upon the growers. It absolutely had to be achieved with their support.

Had he not realized this himself, Roger Plassard would have made it clear to him. By this time, the former organizer for the regional young farmers' association had been working with André Hériard Dubreuil for two years. The two men had had the opportunity to appreciate each other's qualities several years earlier, when they met at the first official eau-de-vie price-setting exercise conducted by the cognac industry. On this occasion, one had represented the merchants; the other, the winegrowers.

Together they successfully put the past behind them, a time not so long ago when a handful of merchants had set eau-de-vie prices in December of each year, at the Cognac fair.

This was not only the start of a new relationship between winegrowers and merchants; it was also the start of a long collaboration between two men who shared the same vision for cognac. When Roger Plassard decided to study the economics of the cognac industry, everyone thought his idea was far-fetched—everyone, that is, except André Hériard Dubreuil. He immediately took on this remarkable winegrower, a graduate of the prestigious HEC Paris business school.

In 1965, Roger Plassard's work took a new dimension. Statistics seemed fairly uninspiring compared to the other job the head of Rémy Martin had assigned him, which was to manage the relationships between the company and the winegrowers. His past experience as a unionist in the farming industry, his easy rapport with people, and the support of André Hériard Dubreuil were convincing reasons to take on this highly sensitive mission, at a time of mounting tension between the winegrowers and the merchants.

The risk of shortage was genuine. If the growth of the cognac market continued at the same pace, the existing vineyards would be unable

The Dutch then encouraged the Charente growers to distill their wine to make *brandewijn*, which the English called brandy, which was more stable and took up less space. This liquor was then diluted with water; it was a boon for both the traders and sailors.

André Hériard Dubreuil during a tasting session in Cognac in 1968.

to meet demand. But as prices continued to fall, the growers had no reason to plant new vines. Then why not motivate them by devising a more equitable division of profits? André Hériard Dubreuil and Roger Plassard were convinced that this was the key to success. If the riches of cognac were not to dry up, they must be shared. They then proposed a truly revolutionary idea to the growers: a contractual arrangement, whereby Rémy Martin would agree to buy eau-de-vie from the producers, according to terms and conditions defined several years in advance.

> **THEY WERE CONVINCED THAT THIS WAS THE KEY TO SUCCESS. IF THE RICHES OF COGNAC WERE NOT TO DRY UP, THEY MUST BE SHARED.**

"We are just like two departments of the same company," insisted Roger Plassard again and again to the growers. "You are the production department; we are the sales department. One cannot function without the other, so let's work together."

They went from one cooperative to another, sometimes from one vineyard to the next, explaining their plan. If Rémy Martin was to continue as both a merchant and producer of cognac, supplies would have to come from within the strict confines of the Grande and Petite Champagne crus. The company also had to carry considerable stocks. For each bottle sold there had to be the equivalent of eight more in the storehouse, and every expected increase in the market had to be backed by a proportionate increase in these stocks.

The brand also had to allocate a large share of its sales to promoting its products, and resources were not limitless. This led to the idea of sharing the financial burden. If the vineyard owners would cover part of the cost of stocks, Rémy Martin could focus its funds on marketing. This was fair, because the winegrowers would benefit from higher prices, and while they were linked to the merchant, they were nevertheless not handcuffed. Each grower could determine the annual volume they would set aside for Rémy Martin, while keeping part of their harvest for direct sale to other customers.

The idea was a simple one, but it took hours of discussions to get the message across, because resistance was strong. It came from the other merchants, of course. That one of their own number would choose to deal with the winegrowers on an equal footing was inconceivable to many of these merchants: a dangerous heresy, pure Bolshevism. There was mistrust in the vineyard owners' camp as well. If there's one thing farmers defend to the bitter end,

EXPERIMENTING WITH A NEW TECHNIQUE. The first alembic worthy of the name came from the Arabs, although descriptions can be found in both classical Greek and Phoenician texts. The etymology itself attests to its cross-border nature: the word "alembic" comes from the Arabic *al-'anbīq*, meaning distillation vessel, itself borrowed from the Greek *ambix*.

it's their independence. Now the merchants wanted to impose their rules? If they signed this supply contract with Rémy Martin, what would become of their freedom? Many feared a trap, and their doubts were naturally fueled by the other merchants. Rémy Martin was accused of trying to reduce the growers to a state of serfdom. Hostile slogans—including "Contract: Theft"—appeared on walls throughout the Charente region.

But André Hériard Dubreuil and Roger Plassard were not to be deterred. They were encouraged rather than dismayed by the objections of the other merchants. The real need was to convince the growers that there was no trap, no deception. They spent months at this task, and finally the idea caught on. The contract was not a piece of thievery; on the contrary, it meant guaranteed revenue for each grower.

By 1965, a number of eau-de-vie distillers had also begun to express interest in the plan, and signed their first contracts with Rémy Martin. During the winter of 1965–66, a considerable number of grower associations were formed, and Rémy Martin immediately supported them. Another important step was taken in 1966, with the formation of the Champaco storage cooperative, under the chairmanship of the ebullient Paul Hosteing. Members of the cooperative were protected by a performance bond, and the first contract with Rémy Martin was for 10,000 hectoliters, from 250 different growers. It was a modest start, but a start nevertheless. For the first time, a cognac brand and a group of growers had decided to work together for several consecutive years.

Roger Plassard, one of the architects of the contractual policy between Rémy Martin and the winegrowers.

Twenty years after the formation of the Champaco cooperative, as many as 2,000 growers, representing production from 20,000 acres (8,000 hectares) of vines, were working with Rémy Martin. Some distilled their own harvests, while others supplied wine to the twenty or so distillers approved by Rémy Martin and Champaco. The company had its own vines in Grande Champagne and its own distillery. But Rémy Martin had always refrained from operating the latter commercially, and did not distil for other growers. Any gain in productivity would have meant a loss of variety. The depth of the Rémy Martin cognacs came in part

Indeed, "alcohol" also comes from the Arabic word *al-kuhl*, initially referring to the kohl, or antimony powder that Egyptian women used as eye makeup. It was then transformed by alchemists to designate the "spirit of wine"—in other words, ethanol, and by extension, all alcoholic beverages.

ONE OF THE GREATS OF COGNAC

from the blend in the same bottle of eaux-de-vie from different distillers. For his part, André Hériard Dubreuil had never sought an exclusive arrangement with Champaco. In the years after the cooperative was formed, it signed contracts with more than a dozen merchants. This was no source of concern to Rémy Martin, as the house had never set out to create a monopoly. Champaco had been established to safeguard the source of supplies and to reduce the burden of investment in stocks. If others wished to follow their example, all the better. The goal had been to encourage growers to stay in business, and this would only accelerate the process.

Not everyone in Cognac was thrilled by the success of Champaco and of Rémy Martin. Revered inside the company and envied outside it, André Hériard Dubreuil was met with hostility from many of his competitors. He was breaking all the rules, and yet forging ahead with confidence. In a small town like Cognac, this was enough to trigger antagonism. The pressure on the growers was even greater. Those who had signed contracts with Rémy Martin were warned to expect retaliation. While the brand name of Rémy Martin enabled growers to obtain prices higher than those offered elsewhere, they were also running the risk of losing their other customers.

War was declared, but André Hériard Dubreuil knew he had won the first battle as he acquired allies among the vineyard owners. The importance of this alliance would become clear many decades later, and even more so today. By reestablishing an equilibrium between the merchants and the growers, Rémy Martin had revolutionized the mindset, not only in and around Cognac, but throughout French agriculture. Twenty years before government authorities adopted the same idea, André Hériard Dubreuil had viewed each grower as an entrepreneur committed to a shared goal, rather than a mere supplier of raw materials. The Charente winegrowers remembered this during the worst times of what came to be known as the "cognac war." In their eyes, the contract was first and foremost a moral commitment, then a financial one.

1966 Rémy Martin had secured its sources of supply. It was time to usher in the second phase, with the creation of a modern production unit. Work started on a large building site on the outskirts of Cognac in 1966. This was to become the Merpins Estate. The project had been under consideration for many years, but André Renaud had never given the go-ahead. He who would have been happy to buy up half of the town of Cognac stone by stone had he felt the need, had failed to recognize the importance of grouping his resources on a single site.

The early pot still was nothing more than a tool, used to extract the essence of fragrant flowers. In the thirteenth century, it was Arnaud de Villeneuve, a Catalan doctor who knew everything about healing everyday woes, a part-time alchemist, and worthy successor of Hippocrates, who first had the idea of distilling not flowers but wine.

André Hériard Dubreuil held a different view. He had no use for a random collection of storehouses. He needed an organized, efficient base; an efficient site from which to grow. Initially,

The impressive Merpins Estate viewed from above.

only twelve storehouses were built, but future extensions were planned, to include up to twenty-five and thirty buildings when complete. It was a modern complex, but designed strictly in accordance with traditional building techniques. The walls were made of local stone, and the earth floor, composed of tightly packed particles of limestone, was left bare to let the natural humidity do its work.

Many people in the region mocked the director of Rémy Martin and his delusions of grandeur. History, however, would show that he demonstrated remarkable foresight. The company employed a staff of 250, but André Hériard Dubreuil already had plans to double his workforce. If was crucial for a cognac producer to be ahead of its time. Anyone who wasn't would fall behind. Nonetheless, André Hériard Dubreuil made no claims to be a visionary. "You just need to know how to read the numbers," he said, dryly.

The new production facility, planned long before the sharp increase in world cognac sales, was ready by the late 1960s. Merpins was not just a modern production unit, it was a symbol designed to show one and all that the Rémy Martin family business had come of age.

> **MANY PEOPLE IN THE REGION MOCKED THE DIRECTOR OF RÉMY MARTIN AND HIS DELUSIONS OF GRANDEUR. HISTORY, HOWEVER, WOULD SHOW THAT HE DEMONSTRATED REMARKABLE FORESIGHT.**

The new centaur, sculpted in 1962 by Otto Quien's sister, Clara, was an apt symbol for the spectacular race that was about to start. Adopted definitively, the brand's symbol had been rejuvenated. It was more of a thoroughbred and reared a bit higher, and the horse's body now carried the head and broad shoulders of a muscular lifeguard. The duality of the centaur expressed a yin and yang balance that was more harmonious, more in sync with the Fine Champagne cognacs, whose scent is uplifted rather than quenched by the fire of alcohol.

He thus discovered eau-de-vie for the Western world, described as a wonderful medicine, an elixir of youth, and a universal panacea. Chemists and physicists later continued the work of Arnaud de Villeneuve, perfecting the art of distillation as the pot still was improved.

The eaux-de-vie are the essential elements for the Cellar Master's work. The samples are tasted and labeled, forming a catalogue from which he will draw to create his blends.

ONE OF THE GREATS OF COGNAC

An aging cellar on the Merpins Estate: this impressive "sea" of 5,000 barrels represents the equivalent of the annual evaporation on the site.

Its face had become smoother, younger; its expression, calmer. The first centaur had aimed an arrow at the ground, but in a powerful, controlled gesture, its successor brandished a less warlike javelin skyward, symbolizing cognac's expansion throughout the world.

> EARLIER ON, ANDRÉ RENAUD HAD OFTEN SAID THAT THE SOUL OF COGNAC COMES FROM THE VINEYARD, DISTILLATION BEING BUT A MEANS TO REVEAL ITS SOUL.

Expansion would indeed take place. In 1967, the state-controlled industry association, the Bureau National Interprofessionnel du Cognac, asked a team of consultants for long-term projections in demand—stretching to the year 1975. The market had been increasing at an annual rate of 9 percent since the early 1960s, but had it reached a saturation point?

The answer was categorical: the period of growth was not yet over. In global terms, the market would continue to increase by 5 to 6 percent each year. Demand for the finest cognacs could even be expected to rise by 50 percent. Many people were skeptical of these conclusions, but not André Hériard Dubreuil. His intuition had been right again. There would be no recession, but instead, further expansion.

But what would this expansion look like? While others finally acknowledged that sales would grow, the debate over cognac quality, however, had not been resolved. Some merchants still hoped that the appellation regulations, which they felt hampered growth, would be relaxed. As in the distant past of phylloxera, they revived the idea of blending an outsider eau-de-vie with an appellation cognac to create an ersatz cognac, a more "common" eau-de-vie. They argued that this was the only way to avoid the soaring prices that would deter buyers.

André Hériard Dubreuil strongly opposed this view, refusing to countenance a new appellation that would make money off the backs of winegrowers. Earlier on, André Renaud had often said that the soul of cognac comes from the vineyard, distillation being but a means to reveal its soul. Without the appellation that was a guarantee for connoisseur and producer

From Spain, the pot still was imported to Ireland where it produced Irish whisky; to Scotland, where it yielded single malt Scotch whisky; to Scandinavia where it gave birth to aquavit; and to Holland where they made Jenever. But this long journey was just a prelude, preparing the way for the pot still's noblest function, the distillation of wine.

During the complex distillation phase, the Cellar Master carefully monitors all the operations and conducts multiple checks to verify the quality of the eaux-de-vie.

Author Marcel Achard, pianist György Cziffra, dancer
Zizi Jeanmaire and singer Juliette Gréco, four stars
in the ad campaign launched in 1968.

alike, what would become of the cognac houses when they had to compete with the major liquor companies? The power of mass advertising was coming into its own, and huge hype around adulterated products could completely destabilize—or even crush—the cognac market. From his experience with VSOP Fine Champagne, André Hériard Dubreuil was convinced that the market had to expand at the top. Price was not the issue, provided it was justified by exceptional quality.

1970 The appellation controversy finally died down three years later, but it didn't disappear: in 1970 it broke out again, when a number of merchants decided to delete the name "Fine Champagne" from their labels. This blow was aimed at Rémy Martin, but it landed directly on the growers of the two Champagne crus instead, provoking considerable discord. The argument raged in the press. The superiority of Fine Champagne cognac, even its very existence, was under fire. The real target, however, was Rémy Martin VSOP, denounced as a poor compromise between Three Star and the superior qualities. This vehement attack over what appeared to be no more than a question of taste would have been surprising, were it not for the fact that Rémy Martin had established its VSOP Fine Champagne as the benchmark for cognac quality, leaving competitors with no choice except imitation or attack.

Hostilities ceased several months later, at least outwardly, but the resentment would take years to simmer down. And, as predicted years earlier by André Hériard Dubreuil, shortages had appeared. Prices could only rise, particularly in the Grande and Petite Champagne vineyards, where demand was the highest. As the pendulum swung back dramatically, the time had come to plant new vines, but ironi-

cally, growers planted too many vines. Planting licenses were granted more often as a way to acquire allies rather than to meet genuine prospects for sales. Whether it was because of miscalculation or due to a deliberate decision, after complaining bitterly about overproduction in the past, the outlying vineyard districts ended up doing exactly that. Perhaps, for those supporting cheap cognac, it was crucial that the price paid to growers be as low as possible.

Charente growers were quick to adopt distilled wine, and were making brandy, the *eau-de-vie* of Charentes, by the early sixteenth century. Local records from the time note that when the first Dutch traders arrived with their pot stills, they were amazed at the quality of the Charente *wijn*.

ORIGINS

André Hériard Dubreuil stood his ground. The belligerent era of 1970 had shown him he was not alone. He had won the support of the growers and also that of other cognac houses, which agreed with his insistence on terroir. The notion of Fine Champagne, the cornerstone of Rémy Martin's success, stood firm, and was confirmed by a consumer survey. Rémy Martin initiates were unwavering in their appreciation of Fine Champagne cognac. There would be no change in policy. The message—"Rémy Martin is Fine Champagne"—would be driven home for a long as necessary.

> **AT THE END OF THE MEAL THE GUEST OF HONOR WAS PRESENTED WITH THE MOST SYMBOLIC AND MARVELOUS OF GIFTS, THE TITLE TO A LIVING GRAPE VINE.**

The Hériard Dubreuil family proudly promoted this gospel to all their guests. The Grollet Estate, a property in Saint-Même-les-Carrières, was an imposing nineteenth-century mansion that had belonged to André Renaud. In the early 1960s, the family devised an original way of sharing their Grande Champagne treasure with their illustrious visitors. Guests were warmly received, but with no great ceremony, as a reminder that they were indeed in farming country. They were served lamb, roasted on a spit in the great fireplace. At the end of the meal the guest of honor was presented with the most symbolic and marvelous of gifts, the title to a living grape vine, which would be marked ceremoniously with a medal. Visitors from the city were loaned boots when the ground was too wet.

Each owner of a minute plot of the Rémy Martin vineyards could come back to follow the progress of "their" vine. If they didn't have time to do this, they received news via an annual

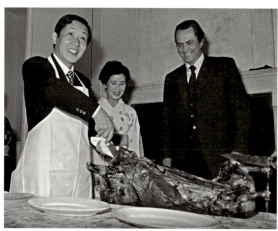
Everyone receives a warm welcome at Le Grollet.

newsletter reporting on the harvest, with commentaries on the economic situation and the vineyard's prospects. Included with the letter was a check, representing net revenue from their grape vine—between ten and eighty centimes, depending on how well the year had been. Thoughtful of their friends, Rémy Martin did not declare these "generous" dividend payments to the tax authorities.

Unlike the eau-de-vie produced elsewhere, where the liquors were so unpalatable that they had to be heavily flavored to be drinkable, the quality of this brandy surpassed anything that had gone before. Sixteenth-century distillers could not have known that this marked the beginning of cognac. They made the best, most highly prized brandy, but it was still just a brandy.

But offering grape vines to illustrious friends was not enough to spread the renown of Rémy Martin cognac. A more in-depth analysis of consumer motivation showed that modernizing the company had not affected its reputation for quality.

> RELOCALIZED OR NOT, THE HOUSE OF RÉMY MARTIN WAS STILL REGARDED AS AN ARDENT DEFENDER OF COGNAC TRADITIONS.

Patrick Quien, international spokesman from 1964 to 1998.

Relocalized or not, the house of Rémy Martin was still regarded as an ardent defender of cognac traditions. But times had changed, supermarket sales were growing, and sales volumes in general were such that brand communication also had to be ramped up. In a word, it was time for a marketing strategy, a term not popular in the region. The very sound of the phrase seemed to evoke a detergent salesman rather than a cognac merchant, for whom the only admissible form of sales promotion had long been the distribution of samples.

The company was on the brink of a cultural revolution. From this point on, a share of the profits was slated to commercial resources designed to boost brand image and create new sales outlets. Earlier practices, when all profits went to purchasing eau-de-vie stocks, were definitively relegated to the past. The most clear-sighted merchants had seen this coming as far back as 1968. In that year, Patrick Quien, who had inherited his father's rare gift of being able to promote cognac in such a way as to win over even the most reticent of customers, had created a public relations department. Another young man joined the company at about this same time, with a title that would have horrified André Renaud: Jacky Paquet was appointed Rémy Martin's Advertising and Promotions Manager.

Meanwhile the detergent salesmen, harbingers of a new era who were both scorned and feared, were making inroads. One of them joined Rémy Martin in 1970, a fox allowed into the henhouse. His name was Yves Blanchard; he arrived straight from Procter & Gamble, one

THE COGNAC EXPERTISE. The secret of cognac—double distillation—had not yet been discovered. This happened in the early seventeenth century with the Chevalier de la Croix Maron, who lived near Segonzac in the Grande Champagne cru. According to legend, he had a dream in which a voice instructed him to distill his wine twice. The second distillation was to refine the results of the first. And with that, Charente-style distilling was born.

André Hériard Dubreuil gifting a vine to his guests at Le Grollet.

of the multinationals whose very name shook up everyone in the cellars. As Marketing and Sales Manager, he took on a key position in the company. After acquiring a modern production unit, the house of Rémy Martin established a forward-looking sales policy.

> THIS BOTTLE HAD ANOTHER ASSET : ITS FROSTED GLASS. BY CASTING A VEIL OF MODESTY OVER THE COGNAC, IT BECAME MORE DESIRABLE.

1972 While the first surveys conducted by the new advertising department confirmed Rémy Martin's exceptional reputation for its cognac, they also identified a weakness—it did not have the bottle it deserved. Yet there could be no question of radically changing the VSOP image, which had been acquired at such cost. The requirements of market expansion were at odds with maintaining tradition, so a compromise had to be found. This was the problem André Hériard Dubreuil asked Yves Blanchard to solve.

"Revamp the bottle, if you have to. But don't change the shape or the color!"

This was akin to squaring a circle, but Yves Blanchard took on the challenge. He produced a bottle that was discreet, true to tradition, elegant, and with just enough roundness not to appear too slender. It was a bold but unpretentious bottle, its only finery a gold label. Its predecessor, inadvertently featuring the white color that is associated with mourning in Asian markets, soon disappeared. This bottle had another asset: its frosted glass. By casting a veil of modesty over the cognac, it became more desirable. When interviewed, customers admitted that they were prepared to pay a higher price for this bottle—which they insisted contained an older cognac—than for a traditional VSOP cognac.

Yves Blanchard was convinced that the frosted bottle would contribute to the success of the Rémy Martin house and its VSOP. Yet he could not have foreseen the impact it would have in the cognac market. The company didn't even need to promote the new bottle; it was soon the only one the public wanted. Rémy Martin's German distributor first refused it, but soon discovered that he would have to sell the new product to meet customer demand. Frosted or not, a bottle would not revolutionize the market on its own, but it could act as a catalyst. And that was exactly what happened. From Cognac to Hong Kong, New York to Tokyo, it conquered the market in less time than it took Yves Blanchard to set up his elite sales team. The globetrotter Otto Quien, who had died in 1970, was succeeded by a team of area managers. They divided up the world market, supervising

The story goes that the Chevalier de la Croix Maron took his discovery to the monks of Renorville near Angles. He brought two casks: the first was drunk immediately; the second was hidden away in the cellar to be saved for a major occasion. This finally took place fifteen years later, with the visit from the Bishop from the town of Saintes.

Advertisement that appeared in Hong Kong in 1975:
"Open a bottle of Rémy Martin and beautiful things will happen." The frosted glass satin VSOP bottle, 1972 (left).

distributors and providing support for their promotional efforts. History was repeating itself. By the time the competition realized the value of the new bottle, Rémy Martin was already far ahead. Just as VSOP was associated with the name of Rémy Martin, the frosted bottle was firmly linked with the same brand. Over the subsequent five or six years, Rémy Martin tripled its market share, and by 1978, had become a full-fledged member of the "Big Four" cognac houses. Rémy Martin owed this status to its exceptional production facility and to its VSOP Fine Champagne. A share of this success can also be credited to the odd, misty bottle with its intriguing, indeed irresistible, allure.

IT WAS TIME FOR RÉMY MARTIN TO CLAIM ITS PLACE AMONG THE BIG PLAYERS.

By 1973, Rémy Martin sales had doubled from 1969. Stocks represented the equivalent of fifty million bottles, or ten times annual sales. Despite an extraordinary rate of growth, Rémy Martin had succeeded in preserving its financial independence. Shortly before celebrating its 250th anniversary, the house of Rémy Martin could lay claim to one-tenth of the total world market. It was time to diversify, notably into champagne, and for Rémy Martin to claim its place among the big players. The celebrations for the 250th anniversary of the house, in 1974, provided André Hériard Dubreuil with the opportunity to do just that—and alongside him, his eldest child, Michel, who had just returned from America to work with his father. Michel Hériard Dubreuil was still in his twenties, but had already launched an impressive career. After studying at the prestigious Wharton business school in Pennsylvania, he was managing the Brazilian subsidiary of the tobacco company Ligget & Myers when his father called him back to France.

1974 Yves Blanchard, responsible for organizing the festivities, gave his colleagues simple instructions: he wanted "an event everyone would remember for the rest of their lives." This challenge was accepted and met. Fifty years later, everyone present still had a crystal clear memory of the party. The high point of the anniversary, attended by three to four hundred salesmen from the international network, was a three-day trip to Venice. From there, they boarded three airplanes, chartered specially for a surprise destination, which turned out to be the Cognac air base, where they were taken to the Merpins cellars for an immense banquet. At the end of the meal, the Hong Kong agent received an even greater surprise—he was rewarded for having exceeded the symbolic threshold of 100,000 cases sold the previous

---

The first surprise—the cask was no longer full, evaporation had done its work—was followed by a revelation. The eau-de-vie had changed color and acquired a new taste, mellowing and growing richer at the same time. This was the true birth of cognac, coinciding with the discovery of oak-cask aging. The Chevalier de la Croix Maron had died long before, and the authenticity of this tale is perhaps debatable, but the moral of the story is not. A true Charentais drinks the cognac of his father, and distills cognac for his son.

year. His emotion and tears were shared by all when his prize appeared on one of the cellar's loading docks: a shiny new Jaguar.

After fêting the sales staff, the following days focused on the winegrowers, who had also been invited to Merpins for the celebrations. They were greeted by the Republican Guard cavalry on horseback, which had arrived from Paris aboard two special train convoys. These festivities may have taken people aback and even appeared ostentatious, but they were meant to mark a symbolic step, a proclamation that times had changed.

As evidenced by the prestigious vintage specially created for the company's 250th anniversary, high-quality products were the order of the day. The challenge that needed to be addressed was not one of supply (secured by contracts with the growers), nor of production (the Merpins Estate took care of that). The problem lay elsewhere. Over the years, VSOP Fine Champagne had become the market reference, opening the door to other superior quality products. A gap had emerged between VSOP Fine Champagne and Louis XIII, by definition an absolutely unrivaled cognac. This gap was mainly due to the Japanese market, where VSOP was no longer considered good enough; they wanted something even better.

Sumptuous banquet in the cellars to celebrate Rémy Martin's 250th year.

Rémy Martin had been selling a cognac called "Âge Inconnu," which in fact met this demand, since 1967. Customers were not interested, however, and a string of name changes—"Lacet d'Or," "Vieille Réserve," then "Grande Réserve"—failed to win it a place in the market. Strangely enough, it only sold well in two or three duty-free stores in which the shopkeeper had added an extra something to the display shelf: an eye-catching card that read "Napoleon" in Japanese.

The primitive Dutch pot still would be improved beyond recognition by successive generations of coppersmiths. In the space of under two centuries, they devised a wondrous piece of equipment, the Charentais pot still. Hammered to perfection on the outside and polished to a mirror finish on the inside, the pot still is made today just as it was long ago.

ORIGINS

Michel Hériard Dubreuil (1945–2012).

So Rémy Martin marketed its own Napoleon. The compromise was in the name, not in the product.

There was one problem, however: by selling a Napoleon cognac, Rémy Martin was entering the competitive arena, so the quality of the product needed the support of outstanding packaging. The designer selected for this task set to work immediately. He prepared five or six suggestions, but there was one he worked on more or less secretly, and in which he never lost faith despite André Hériard Dubreuil's reservations. His perseverance was rewarded. This special box with its gold-accented red cameo set the Napoleon cognac apart from the VSOP Fine Champagne cognac, which it did not disown but simply transcended. It was successful beyond the company's wildest hopes; Rémy Martin may not have changed the Japanese mindset, but it certainly won a new commercial challenge.

What was to be done? Napoleon was all the rage. The name had been introduced after the phylloxera epidemic, to identify pre-phylloxera cognacs made from wines produced under Napoleon III. The name no longer had any precise connotation, and the figure of Napoleon III had been replaced by that of his uncle, Napoleon Bonaparte. Should a campaign be run to explain that a "Lacet d'Or" was worth as much, or more, than a Napoleon? André Hériard Dubreuil decided against such a strategy, considering it "easier to change a label than the mentality of the Japanese."

André and Anne-Marie Hériard Dubreuil at the 250th anniversary.

No cognac house would ever employ a distiller without first taking a very close look at the type of stills he used, and the cleanliness of his distillery. This is not, by the way, incompatible with an innovative approach, as for example, when electronics and sensors are incorporated to support traditional techniques.

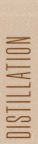

DISTILLATION

ONE OF THE GREATS OF COGNAC

> AFTER A SERIES OF EXTENSIONS, THE IMPRESSIVE FIFTY ACRES OF CELLARS ON THE MERPINS ESTATE NOW HOUSED THE LARGEST STOCK OF FINE CHAMPAGNE COGNAC EVER.

At the age of fifty-seven, André Hériard Dubreuil could be well satisfied with his achievements. André Renaud had enhanced the brand created by Rémy Martin with an unconditional respect for the terroir of the Champagne crus and an efficient international sales organization; André Hériard Dubreuil had added security of supply, an effective marketing policy, and admirable financial strength. He had also created a one-of-a-kind production tool. After a series of extensions, the impressive fifty acres (twenty hectares) of cellars on the Merpins Estate now housed the largest stock of Fine Champagne cognac ever: 130,000 barrels of cognac, the equivalent of 160 million bottles.

In 1970, an equally impressive cooperage, the largest in Europe, was built on the Merpins Estate, turning out 30,000 barrels a year—a quarter of total French production. At Seguin Moreau, the cognac barrels were made exclusively from French oak, primarily from the Limousin region, as it is the only wood that allowed the aromas and flavors of the cognac to develop freely. The wood was left to season for three years in a fifteen-acre (six-hectare) open-air timber yard, so that time could alleviate its bitterness. At that point, the Merpins timber stock represented the equivalent of 40,000 Limousin oak trees. Like André Renaud, André Hériard Dubreuil attached at least as much importance to the wood as to the eau-de-vie itself. As for André Giraud, the Cellar Master,

DISTILLATION

HARMONY OF THE ELEMENTS. Distillation involves a subtle contact between liquid and copper. This contact develops the finest characteristics of the wine, trapping the fatty acids and sulfur compounds, while allowing the aromas to develop. The smaller the still, the more evenly the heat is distributed and the better the contact. This is why Rémy Martin never loads its stills with more than 25 hectoliters, although according to regulations, stills for the first distillation are allowed to contain 140 hectoliters of wine.

he had no hesitation in tasting the wood, conscientiously chewing away on shards to make sure it was ready.

All that remained was to consolidate the positions won and gain a further slice of an ever-increasing market, year by year, but the work was not yet done. André Hériard Dubreuil turned his attention to the only link in the chain that was not in his full control: the distribution network. Rémy Martin had certainly progressed since the epic days of the Swiss subsidiary. After France, Germany, and Belgium, subsidiaries had also been founded in Britain and the Netherlands; the company had even taken over its Australian distributor. Nevertheless, the situation was still unclear in several countries, and particularly in Asia. The agents might well be associated with Rémy Martin, but they were not Rémy Martin. Although the ties with Cognac were strong, the importers were still masters of their profits, even to the extent of using them to promote competing products. The distributors had to defend the Rémy Martin brand in their countries just as vigorously as it was defended in Cognac. If the producer doubled his targets, the vendor had to do the same, and be ready to share the financial risks.

When a distributor refused to take part in these expansion plans, Rémy Martin would set up its own subsidiary. This is what happened in Hong Kong, and later in Singapore, Malaysia, Japan, and the United States. The area managers, directing business from Cognac or Paris, handed over responsibility to local managers. Without those subsidiaries, Rémy Martin's plans and policies would have come to nothing and its goals would not have been achieved, but with their support, the company could indulge its passion for cognac to the full, controlling every step of the long path from the vineyards of Champagne to its customers on every continent.

Michel, the elder son of Anne-Marie and André Hériard Dubreuil, played a key role in the creation of the distribution network between 1974 and 1980. Where Yves Blanchard had demonstrated his tactical genius by demonstrating that, beyond the product itself, cognac lived by its image, Michel Hériard Dubreuil proved his sense of strategy by directing the diversification of Rémy Martin. He formed a team for this purpose, and recruited Peter Sosnkowski, who in turn would call on Ralph Browning—originally, like himself, from the Procter & Gamble empire. Years later, Ralph Browning and Peter Sosnkowski would both become managers of the group they had helped to create. As was also the case with Yves Blanchard, they were not just part of a new generation of executives joining the company; they also represented the new culture that was taking root, cementing the bond between cognac and marketing.

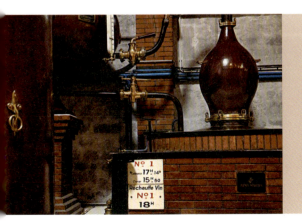

DISTILLATION

Charente distillers employ much the same methods, whether they distill their own wine or work for other growers. Twenty-five hectoliters of a wine containing an alcohol content of about 8 degrees alcohol yields less than 3 hectoliters of an eau-de-vie of 70 degrees alcohol. If the rules of the art are followed with care, the eau-de-vie contains all the aromas and flavors which, under the hand of the Cellar Master and his or her ally—time—will one day become a splendid cognac.

ONE OF THE GREATS OF COGNAC

The toasting process involves heating the barrels a second time to release the aromas of the wood.

A croze is used to cut the grooves inside of the casks, on the ends to which the heads are fitted.

The results were not long in coming. Rémy Martin gained ground year by year. A mere fourth of the leading cognac houses in 1972, the company tripled its market share in just four years, and the increase was even stronger in the late 1970s. In the space of two years, staff numbers at Cognac doubled, growing from 250 to 500 people. The house was expanding, but Anne-Marie and André Hériard Dubreuil preserved its family spirit. They remained easily approachable, always knowing what to say to reassure, motivate, or comfort someone. Winegrowers and ambassadors were greeted with the same open-mindedness, listened to with the same respect. This was not mere posturing on their part; it was their natural behavior. And although André Hériard Dubreuil was the boss, his wife Anne-Marie personified the soul of the company. Discreet but ever-present, she was a considerate personnel manager and a public relations maestro. Born in Charente, she was also a grande dame of cognac, heir to the tax privileges of distillers, and, above all, an outstanding taster. Many visitors were struck by her impassioned descriptions of eau-de-vie from the Grande Champagne cru.

The cognac market was changing, however, and Peter Sosnkowski was sent to the United States to set up a subsidiary and revamp the Rémy Martin brand image. With the active involvement of Bob Beleson, the brand was relaunched in the United States under the simple first name "Rémy". It ventured beyond the inside pages of its usual serious daily papers to be brazenly displayed on bus shelters, and from Beverly Hills to Manhattan, "Rémy" became the rallying call of a prosperous new generation and anyone who identified with it. Rémy Martin cognac with soda, previously considered sacrilegious, became the "in" drink of the day.

Rémy Martin had two reference points: VSOP and Louis XIII. Between the two, the Napoleon cognac had conquered the Japanese market, which was becoming increasingly demanding, insisting on greater age, delicacy, subtlety, and personality. The great cognacs—unsellable a few years earlier, except in minute quantities—became increasingly sought-after. Rémy Martin had to meet this demand without harming the VSOP Fine Champagne on which its international reputation was established, and without losing the individuality and specific flavors of its cognac. There was no question of producing a "super-VSOP," and even less of venturing into an area where Rémy Martin would lose its very soul. What was needed was a quality between VSOP and Louis XIII, based on the same identity, or structure. At the instigation of Ralph Browning, a new family of cognacs was to come into being—the "Qualité Supérieure Supérieure" or "QSS," in which all the individuals were created harmoniously and each had its own personality.

DISTILLATION

Placed over the open flame of a brick hearth, the boiler is shaped like a flat-bottomed bowl, whose sides gradually thin out to ensure even heating. The bowl is covered with a dome and capped with an onion-shaped bulb through which the vapors rise into the swan neck. They then pass through a long tube into the condenser coil, encased in its cooling shaft. This is where the first distillate, known as the *brouillis*, is collected. The *brouillis* is redistilled, producing the eau-de-vie.

Ad campaign for the United States, 1981.

ONE OF THE GREATS OF COGNAC

Tasting eaux-de-vie and cognac is a three-step process that begins with a visual examination, followed by an olfactory analysis and finally, the actual tasting.

André Hériard Dubreuil, who had a scientific background, was an expert taster. The time had come for researchers to analyze, explain, and master what generations of Cellar Masters had known by instinct. So in 1972, he put together a small research team that worked behind the scenes to discover cognac's most intimate, molecular secrets. The team was first set up at a discreet distance, in Toulouse, then in 1976 it moved to the Merpins Estate to continue its circumspect work. Year after year, it carried out multiple tests in its quest to answer an almost sacrilegious question: what chemical characteristics make one eau-de-vie more or less flavorful than another? It was time to move on to the next stage: André Hériard Dubreuil asked his small team of enthusiastic researchers and professionals to work with the Cellar Master on standardizing the future QSS range, each note of which had to be perfectly balanced. For the first time, a cognac house was associating a team of scientists on a key production mission.

Robert Léauté, the head of the Rémy Martin laboratory, accepted eagerly. After working for several years alongside Cellar Master André Giraud, he had learned the taste and style of the Rémy Martin brand. He had not forgotten his hair-raising initiation when he joined the company in 1973: a tasting session with André Hériard Dubreuil and André Giraud. Nothing could have been more terrifying for the new enologist than finding himself confronted with two master tasters, one representing the house, the other the cellars. André Renaud had assigned André Giraud to this post because the latter had once detected an imperceptible trace of fuel oil in an eau-de-vie—the result of an unfortunate technical problem that had befallen one of the growers. As for André Hériard Dubreuil, his nose was said to be as good as his father-in-law's. They handed Robert Léauté a glass:

"What do you think of this eau-de-vie?"
For a moment, Robert Léauté tried to read his interrogators' minds, looking for the slightest clue to the right answer. But they were giving nothing away, so he opted for honesty:
"I'm sorry," he answered, "but I find it oily and heavy."
"Nevertheless, that's the one we need!" came the two experts' amused reply.

Although incongruous at first taste, the roughness of the eau-de-vie constituted the very structure of Rémy Martin cognac, which revealed its true qualities with age, not in the first years. André Giraud and André Hériard Dubreuil invited the young enologist to experience that for himself. He chose what he thought was the most elegant eau-de-vie, which was then clearly marked and left to undergo the test of time. After only one year, the eau-de-vie he

During vinification, the grape yeast, mixed with minute particles of fruit, settles in the bottom of the vat, where it forms the all-important lees. Crucial to the aging process, these lees contribute to the complexity of the "rancio," or nutty fragrance typical of great aged cognacs.

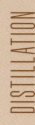

had chosen had lost its flavor, while the one that André Giraud and André Hériard Dubreuil had given him to taste had improved.

> EACH DISTILLER LEAVES HIS PARTICULAR MARK, EACH YEAR CONTRIBUTES ITS PARTICULAR CHARACTER, EACH VINE HAS ITS OWN QUALITIES. THE CELLAR MASTER HAS TO ACHIEVE HARMONY FROM THIS PROFUSION BY CONTINUOUS BLENDING.

Every Rémy Martin cognac features this structure, characteristic of the Fine Champagne, with its crescendo of aromas and flavors. Unlike certain "monolithic" blends, which always have a dominant characteristic, the Rémy Martin style is reflected in the distinct diversity of its eaux-de-vie. Each distiller leaves his particular mark, each year contributes its particular character, each vine has its own qualities. The Cellar Master has to achieve harmony from this profusion by continuous blending. The apotheosis of the brand—Louis XIII—contains countless eaux-de-vie from Grande Champagne.

Such a blending process, no matter how empirical, cannot be improvised. Before the blend is made, the blender has to know what it will produce in ten or twenty years' time. That kind of knowledge cannot be invented, only handed down from master to pupil. It was the particular artistry of André Giraud, and would be that of his successor, Georges Clot. The Cellar Master's intuition was recognized as all-important, but the different stages in the life of a cognac were as yet improperly understood. The laboratory began to examine this question, and its intensive research resulted in an unprecedented "genetic mapping" of cognac, featuring 450 basic elements over the different stages of the aging process. The tool was so precise that it would later be adopted by the Bureau National Interprofessionnel du Cognac (BNIC) industry association, and even by the official French fraud control department, to detect any cheating with regard to a product's age.

The researchers discovered that, in addition to the VSOP, four ages could be clearly identified. The first reflects the ardor of youth combined with the power of adolescence. After twelve to fifteen years, with the beginnings of oxidation, the wood releases the aromas of dried fruit, and scents akin to those of port, Madeira, and sherry can be distinguished. During the second stage, the cognac softens, giving a hint of saffron and jasmine, but it is not truly adult until it has aged for thirty or forty years.

Distillation on the lees is not obligatory; some prefer to skip this. But not Rémy Martin's suppliers, who keep their wine on its lees after fermentation to boost the aromatic potential. Distillation of wine on the lees gives the cognac more body and more power, and a longer finish. But there is no room for error. Only small stills, ensuring even heating, can be used, and the flame has to be closely monitored, as the lees cannot withstand too much heat; burnt lees produce an unpalatable smoky taste known as *rimé*.

A selection of new, unmarked eaux-de-vie in the tasting room.
Adding water reveals their aromatic potential and potential for aging.

In its prime, the eau-de-vie grows rounder, adding a suggestion of mature Muscat grapes to its range of flavors. The odor of the wood has also undergone a metamorphosis, now approaching that of a cigar box. This third stage corresponds to a Fine Champagne cognac at its peak.

> **VERY FEW COGNACS ATTAIN SUCH SOPHISTICATION, WHICH IS ONLY ACQUIRED AFTER FORTY-FIVE OR FIFTY-FIVE YEARS. ONLY THE COGNACS OF GRANDE CHAMPAGNE RELEASE THEIR AROMAS WITH SUCH POWER AND PRECISION.**

Beyond this is the holy of holies, the kingdom reserved for the very greatest. Very few cognacs attain such sophistication, which is only acquired after forty-five or fifty-five years. Only the cognacs of Grande Champagne release their aromas with such power and precision. If we consider cognac as "drinkable perfume," this is the subtlest scent, suggestive of exotic fruits, rose, and violet. The wood has become sandalwood, and the taste lingers in the mouth for more than an hour.

1981

The QSS range of cognacs was founded on those four stages: the Napoleon, then XO, followed by Extra, with Louis XIII standing alone at the top. Fine Champagne is the base, with Grande Champagne growing in importance toward the top of the cognac ladder of quality. At least half the eaux-de-vie for a VSOP came from the Grande Champagne cru, with the proportion rising to two-thirds for a Napoleon, and about 90 percent for an Extra.

This basic structure would be strictly adhered to, but there were endless possible variations. Blending could be nuanced, the choice of grapes could be varied, the Ugni Blanc grape could be combined with the pastoral tones of the Colombard or the floral hints of the Folle Blanche. The composition of the cognac could be further refined by using younger or older barrels, according to the strength of aroma required. But the style was set, as in the world of high fashion, with golden rules on which there was no compromise. The wines were always distilled on their lees, with the yeasts fixing the aromas and protecting the palate from the roughness of the alcohol. The copper stills never held more than 25 hectoliters, ensuring the best possible contact between the liquid and the heat source. And all the storehouses in which the cognac was left to age, with bare earth floors which let the humidity seep through, were built of local stone.

DISTILLATION

ATTENTION AND INTUITION. Distillation temperatures must be carefully monitored, with thermometers, of course, and by the distiller himself. The wine can be slightly warmed before it is poured into the boiler, at the start of the actual distillation process.

THE SPIRIT OF COGNAC

Ritual of service of Louis XIII cognac in the 1980s.

All this did not stem from some kind of company folklore or misplaced conservatism; it merely reflected a desire to conform to a certain taste and produce a cognac recognizable among thousands, one that was true to the essence of the Rémy Martin cognacs sold at the beginning of the century. André Hériard Dubreuil coined a phrase that he often used to summarize this approach: "If there is just one customer in the whole world who can recognize my product, I'll make it for him!"

As a result, the brand now had millions of customers. And rather than a mere alignment of products corresponding to price and market segments, the brand range itself represented a history of cognac. If Rémy Martin chose to sell eaux-de-vie that were much older than required by the regulations, it was not for marketing reasons; it was simply the practical application of principles revealed by his laboratory, bolstering over 250 years of experience accumulated by successive generations of winegrowers and distillers.

André Hériard Dubreuil turned sixty-five in 1982. He had one last challenge to address: preparing his succession at the head of the company. His oldest son Michel had decided to withdraw for health reasons, so the chairmanship was passed to Michel's two brothers, François and Marc. The former, a mathematician by training and a graduate of the INSEAD business school, joined Rémy Martin in 1977. Such a move was not part of his career plan; he had a job he loved in a completely different sector, one that frequently took him abroad, but his father found the weak point in the situation. Adopting a ploy that might have appealed to André Renaud, André Hériard Dubreuil did not attempt to convince his son, but suggested to his daughter-in-law, Dominique, "If François joins the company, you won't have to keep moving all the time."

The young couple already had two children, and had moved eight times in the space of a few years. The argument hit home. The next day, François Hériard Dubreuil accepted his father's offer, on one condition: that his brother Marc come along too. The latter, his junior by three years, was a graduate of the ESSEC business school and was working in marketing for an American group; he was also a new father. Like his older brother, Marc had never imagined working for Rémy Martin, but he also accepted, and joined the company the following year. This was the start of an extraordinary duo that lasted for decades and never faltered. The brothers made no bones about their differences, but were interchangeable when necessary. Differing views were confronted and compared for as long as necessary, each brother determinedly arguing his side, with the result that they sometimes ended up convinced of the other's point of view.

DISTILLATION

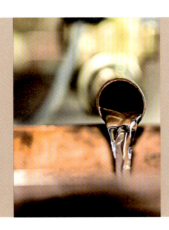

The "heads," or *têtes*, obtained during the early stages of first distillation, are aggressive and heavy, they are separated and recycled in the undistilled wine. The final product of first distillation, the *brouillis*, must be filtered with extreme care as it drains out of the still. This process takes about eight hours. After this, the distillate loses its strength and again contains undesirable components. These are the "tails," or *queues*, which are also separated for later redistillation.

François and Marc Hériard Dubreuil had no intention of restricting themselves to the role of passive heirs. Instead, they initiated a project as bold, grandiose, and extraordinary as that of their father and grandfather. Rémy Martin, originally a small merchant house in Rouillac, which had gone on to earn a place among the great cognac houses, would now become a global giant in the distribution of quality wines and liquors. To reach this goal, it was not enough to control a distribution network: the network had to make profits, and the Rémy Martin brand, no matter how prestigious, could not achieve this alone. The subsidiaries on every continent would have to sell other products. André Hériard Dubreuil, who had reached this conclusion in the 1970s, had bought up a number of renowned French liquor brands; his sons would go much further, and much faster, even if it meant a few sleepless nights for the company's bankers. In May 1983, they founded Rémy Martin International, followed in 1986 by Rémy & Associés, a wine and liquor group that went far beyond cognac.

Anne-Marie and André Hériard Dubreuil, surrounded by their children, François, Marc, and Dominique, in the gardens of Le Grollet.

From the Grande and Petite Champagne vineyards around Cognac, the group set out to conquer the other Champagne, near Reims in northeastern France, with its famous sparkling wine. After buying Krug, the only champagne house producing exclusively top-of-the-range vintages, it acquired Charles Heidsieck and Piper-Heidsieck, a family concern with which the company had been doing business for several generations. Rémy Martin also moved into the wine production and business sector, particularly in the Bordeaux region, with De Luze and La Grande Cave, which had a stock of some two million bottles of great Bordeaux vintages. The company was also established in Australia, Brazil, and California, where its wine production maintained the same emphasis on perfection, the same insistence on quality. It even became the producer of a wine renowned in China, the Dynasty, thanks to the intuition of François Hériard Dubreuil who had set up a joint venture with the local authorities there in 1980—only the second collaboration of that type ever to be made with a Western company.

DISTILLATION

Only *brouillis* with 27 to 30 degrees of alcohol from the first distillation will then undergo a second distillation process. This is the *bonne chauffe*; again, only part of the condensate is kept. The têtes are separated and recycled as before. The second distillation yields a clear, bright eau-de-vie of about 70 degrees of alcohol. This liquid, the "heart," or *coeur*, of the cognac, drains off for about five hours until, almost imperceptibly, it starts to weaken.

Cognac was still the group's flagship product, however, thanks in part to the VSOP, but also to the growing success of the QSS cognacs. Launched in 1981, XO increased its market share over the years. Surprisingly enough, its elegant round decanter was the result of a mistake by the glass-maker. In the original mold, the craftsman had turned the notches inward, rather than outward as he had been asked to do. Despite the mistake, the result looked good: the decanter caught the light beautifully and delivered its glow to the cognac. It was therefore decided to keep it—a wise decision, judging by its enduring popularity. Another success story was that of the Club cognac which, in its original octagonal bottle, would become a huge hit in the Asian market. The intuition of the past was resoundingly confirmed: in addition to the VSOP and the Napoleon, a whole new market was there for the taking. At the company's head office in Cognac, a challenge was launched: "When we've sold 200,000 cases of QSS, we'll throw a huge party!"

> LAUNCHED IN 1981, XO INCREASED ITS MARKET SHARE OVER THE YEARS. SURPRISINGLY ENOUGH, ITS ELEGANT ROUND DECANTER WAS THE RESULT OF A MISTAKE BY THE GLASS-MAKER.

1988 That day came far sooner than expected. By 1988, 200,000 cases had been sold and, as promised, a lawn party was held at the Merpins Estate. A special blend was created to mark the occasion: a great cognac with a remarkably long finish, a decanter of which was presented to each guest. Its chosen name, "Défi QSS," was perhaps not very poetic, but was strongly symbolic; moreover, the blend was created in the very first storehouse built on the site in 1966. Those who attended the party were unlikely to forget the moment when André Hériard Dubreuil, officially retired but still present, was preparing to speak. It took him a long time to compose himself, but he was met with a spontaneous standing ovation that seemed it would never end—thunderous applause in recognition of his valiant defense of a certain idea of cognac, his support for cooperation and mutually beneficial practices rather than rivalry and point-scoring, and his loyalty to all the employees and winegrowers with whom he had shared his career. At over seventy years old, this man whose initial training had destined him for a forest management career in North Africa or elsewhere, had eventually devoted his working life to Charente, its vineyards, and its winegrowers. That was well worth a standing ovation, a few emotional tears, and a heartfelt message of gratitude and mutual appreciation.

At Rémy Martin, only a relatively small proportion of the *secondes*, which follows the *coeur*, will be gradually mixed in with the *brouillis*—between 20 and 25 percent of total volume, never more. If the amount is larger, the taste of the *secondes* spoils the cognac. The rest of the *secondes* are returned to the wine, and is run through the complete distillation cycle a second time.

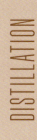

DISTILLATION

One attendee was particularly touched by the scene. Dominique Hériard Dubreuil, the elder sister of François and Marc, was preparing to take over the Rémy Martin house. Like her father and brothers, she had had no intention of joining the family company. She had trained as a jurist and embarked on a successful career in public relations, which she found perfectly satisfying and which, above all, gave her something she considered an essential privilege: total independence. However, after almost a year of reflection, she finally said yes—partly out of filial loyalty, partly because she had a sense of what she could contribute to the brand. She was probably far from imagining the mark she would leave on the cognac house and the liquor group.

> BY THE EARLY 1990S, ALL THE PLAYERS WERE ALIGNED AND READY TO WRITE A NEW CHAPTER IN THE HISTORY OF RÉMY MARTIN, A FAMILY CONCERN IN MORE WAYS THAN ONE.

By the early 1990s, all the players were aligned and ready to write a new chapter in the history of Rémy Martin, a family concern in more ways than one. Jean-Pierre Giraud, whose father, grandfather, and great-grandfather had already worked for the company, became director of Rémy Martin, and the company spokesman was Otto Quien's son, Patrick. At Champaco, the first names of the winegrowers and distillers had changed but the family names (the Roys, Guionnets, Mullons, and Gauthiers) endured, ensuring the continuity of an association initiated by their predecessors. A generational shift also occurred in the storehouses where, in 1990, after three decades of tireless work, André Giraud handed over the keys to his right-hand man, Georges Clot, a highly symbolic change that saw a cooper replaced by an engineer—empiricism giving way to science. Georges Clot was not starting from scratch; he inherited an exceptional stock, patiently compiled by his predecessor. Moreover, a new storehouse had just been built on the edge of the Merpins Estate—an innovative storehouse, designed to hold the oldest eaux-de-vie, the (provisional) result of the visionary project launched some thirty years earlier by André Hériard Dubreuil.

Settled into a family home in Grande Champagne, Dominique Hériard Dubreuil set herself the task of reconciling the age-old traditions of a company founded in 1724 with the realities of a rapidly expanding group. Buoyed by the inspirational sense of belonging to something larger than herself, she gently but firmly imposed her own style. She got her voice heard without raising it, and convinced

DISTILLATION

The distiller's skill is crucial to the selection of the *coeur*. He or she must avoid sudden changes in the rate of flow by adjusting the heat, which slows down the evaporation process during the delicate distillation operation; they must also respect the correct filtering times for the various distillates. These rules are crucial for the gradual selection of the cognac's aromas, and mean that the distillation process requires virtually constant monitoring.

The Club bottle with eight facets was designed with utmost care, earning it an Oscar de l'emballage award in 1986.

without coercing. She got to know each individual and listened attentively to everyone, but her ambitions for the company were clear and she asserted her credo from the start: "We have a fine image; we should bring it fully alive, rigorously and coherently." Gone were the days when a sign at the entrance to the buildings on Rue de la Société-Vinicole read, "The house is not open to visitors." Now, from springtime onward, a little train would take people on a tour of the Merpins Estate. Rémy Martin was embracing its history, its heritage, and its public, all at once.

HER AMBITIONS FOR THE COMPANY WERE CLEAR AND SHE ASSERTED HER CREDO FROM THE START: "WE HAVE A FINE IMAGE; WE SHOULD BRING IT FULLY ALIVE, RIGOROUSLY AND COHERENTLY."

1990 Meanwhile, in their premises on the Champs-Élysées in Paris, François and Marc Hériard Dubreuil had taken over the new liquor group. Having acquired Mount Gay Rum in 1989, they merged with Cointreau in 1990, boosting the group's expansion strategy, and went on to accept a minority shareholding by Britain's Grand Metropolitan conglomerate.

A few months later, the Scottish group Highland Distilleries bought a stake in the Rémy Martin family holding company, and the group expanded its range of quality liquors with Scotch whiskies and single malts.

By Christmas 1991, the new Rémy Cointreau Group owned a full range of cognacs (with a leading position in the QSS category), liquors, champagnes, and still wines. It was worth over six billion French francs, up from one billion just ten years previously. It had twenty-five subsidiaries and a presence in 170 countries, employed over 3,000 people, and was listed on the Paris and Frankfurt stock exchanges. It was like a splendid ship, whose captains were eager to pursue their exploration of the world: to the United States, which was still the top market for cognac, and to Asia, which was driving global growth. Accustomed to the ups and downs of business, François and Marc Hériard Dubreuil knew they would sail into a few storms sooner or later—but they did not know that the first of those storms was already on the horizon, and would be tempestuous indeed.

DISTILLATION

Distillers "play with fire" to achieve the best results from their alembics, drawing from the memory of distillations from the past and relying heavily on their own intuition. Each distiller therefore imparts a distinctive style to their eaux-de-vie, which the Cellar Master is eager to discover as the process is underway.

The Merpins Estate cellars (photographed by Yann Arthus-Bertrand), a highlight for the visitors who discover the estate aboard a train.

Since 1991
TIME
REGAINED

1991 The cognac industry had been focusing on Japan for several years. Buoyed by an extraordinary economic boom, the Japanese archipelago had become the new El Dorado for merchants. Customers in the bars of Tokyo's upscale neighborhood, Ginza, were spending lavishly, and gifts of quality cognac were almost a professional obligation, demonstrating respect for one's guest and the success of one's own company.

The Rémy Martin brand adapted more easily than others to the extraordinary progression of the Japanese market, to which it dedicated specific products such as the VSOP Supérieur, promoted from 1987 by the most prestigious of ambassadors, Alain Delon. On the screen, on posters, in the press, and even on telephone cards, Japan's most popular French actor proclaimed in French, with his irresistible smile, "For me, Rémy Martin is the best." He was highly convincing; in fact, the man and the brand seemed made for each other, expressing the same values of elegance and sophistication, with a certain French *je ne sais quoi* that made them all the more desirable. The partnership with Alain Delon was not the only reason for Rémy Martin's success in Japan, but it certainly contributed to it: 800,000 bottles were sold in 1988, and over 3.5 million only two years later.

> THE MAN AND THE BRAND SEEMED MADE FOR EACH OTHER, EXPRESSING THE SAME VALUES OF ELEGANCE AND SOPHISTICATION, WITH A CERTAIN FRENCH *JE NE SAIS QUOI* THAT MADE THEM ALL THE MORE DESIRABLE.

While the world was bogged down in a strange kind of crisis, and the Gulf War and transatlantic trade disputes were impacting their exports, it was thanks to Japan that the Charente producers saw their sales increase. The country was seen as a reason for optimism, a promise that anything was still possible. As indeed it was—including a catastrophe that occurred without warning at the beginning of 1992. In just a few months, Japan left the conquering 1980s behind and entered the "lost decade" of the 1990s. The overly speculative real estate market collapsed and dragged the stock market

EAU-DE-VIE

Tasting a fresh eau-de-vie is nothing like tasting an aged cognac. It is a much more difficult task, as both the qualities and flaws are still latent. Nevertheless, the Cellar Master—whose skill in predicting how well an eau-de-vie cognac will mature is vital—can be convinced by this first tasting. With assistance from the tasting committee, the Cellar Master makes their selection, which must be made before March 31, at which time the cognacs are given a 00 rating.

Alain Delon, a faithful ambassador for Rémy Martin.

down with it. Major banks failed, industry went into recession, and unemployment and deflation became entrenched.

Over 6,000 miles away, the world of cognac was a collateral victim of this dramatic economic downturn. The shockwave took a while to be felt. The terrible frost of April 21, 1991, which destroyed two-thirds of the region's wine production, paradoxically contributed to temporarily masking something that the drop in the Japanese market would bring to light: despite the uprooting of previous years, the Charente vineyards were still overproducing, inflated by the excessive planting of the 1970s. Almost two decades later, the Japanese crisis merely revealed an underlying issue that had never been resolved.

THE OLDEST, MOST DISTINGUISHED COGNACS WERE THE ONES BEST ABLE TO RESIST THE CRISIS, AND DOMINIQUE HÉRIARD DUBREUIL WAS CONVINCED THAT THEY REPRESENTED THE WAY FORWARD.

As was the case in 1934, 1970, and whenever production exceeded demand, prices fell rapidly. Protected by their contractual agreements, Rémy Martin's traditional suppliers were not the hardest hit. They could still deliver some of their eaux-de-vie at fair prices, but they could not find buyers for the production glut. Unable to finance their stocks, they sold them off cheaply and made even greater losses. Those who had made major investments could no longer repay their loans. This was the flip side of globalization: the bursting of a real-estate bubble in Tokyo could lead to bankruptcy and despair among small winegrowers in the Cognac region.

There were two contrasting strategies for dealing with this crisis. Some thought the market should be left to sort itself out, no matter how painful the process. As global demand was declining, traders should reduce volumes and purchase prices, and try to sell off their stocks in the hope of better days to come. But Rémy Martin, among others, believed that solidarity was essential to get through this difficult period. For the house of Rémy Martin, winegrowers and distillers were not anonymous suppliers, but partners with whom they were on first-name terms, long-standing family friends one might encounter in the vineyards, at meetings, or at tasting sessions. Rémy Martin and Champaco had just celebrated twenty-five years of contractual relations; they should navigate the path to recovery together.

As usual, the process began at the top. The oldest, most distinguished cognacs were the ones best able to resist the crisis, and Dominique Hériard Dubreuil was convinced

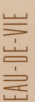

THE TASTING CEREMONY. The tastings, which at Rémy Martin are blind, take place preferably in the late morning. Participants do not know the origins, tasting only numbered eaux-de-vie. They are all assessed anonymously, including those from the house's own estates, so that they are judged solely on objective criteria. According to tradition, any supplier, whether they be a winegrower or distiller, can ask to participate in a tasting session to better understand the subtle, but objective reasons for which one eau-de-vie is rated better than another one.

Dominique Hériard Dubreuil in the 1980s.

that they represented the way forward. As she wrote in the company magazine: "There is nothing to suggest that global sales will pick up significantly in 1993. We will therefore have to redouble our efforts to ensure that Rémy Martin continues to hold its own, be ever more vigilant as to the quality of our products, and ever more united around our company's prime objective: to offer consumers the best eaux-de-vie in the world."

> **AN EXCLUSIVE CIRCLE WHERE, IN ACCORDANCE WITH TRADITION, EXPERTS TASTE, OBSERVE, AND SMELL EACH SAMPLE ANONYMOUSLY BEFORE APPROVING OR REJECTING IT.**

The "best eaux-de-vie in the world"—that was easier said than done, but anyone who knew the president of Rémy Martin would realize that it was not just a figure of speech. On the contrary, it was the linchpin of a strategy to improve the quality and consistency of the eaux-de-vie. To see such a project through, Dominique Hériard Dubreuil knew she could count on Georges Clot, the Cellar Master, and also on Pierrette Trichet, who had replaced him as head of the laboratory.

Originally from the Gers region, the land of Armagnac where her father was a farmer and winegrower and her mother a teacher, Pierrette Trichet had had time to grow accustomed to the world of cognac. She had been working alongside Georges Clot since 1974 and the epic days of the laboratory's launch in Toulouse. She was a hard worker, exceptionally diligent and rigorous, but could often be heard bursting into laughter, because she showed the same enthusiasm and integrity in her work as in her personal life. A chemist by training, she was obsessed with gaining a better understanding of the correlations between tasting and analysis, identifying what occurs on the molecular level when the nose or palate perceives a defect, or, on the contrary, a remarkable quality in an eau-de-vie. To achieve this, she would have to build a bridge between two such radically different places as the tasting committee and the laboratory. On the one hand, an exclusive circle where, in accordance with tradition, experts taste, observe, and smell each sample anonymously before approving or rejecting it; and on the other, the lair of the scientists with their computers and curious machines, chromatographs, and mass spectrometers, whose very names seem an affront to the age-old cognac tradition. However, those two places seemed contradictory only to non-specialists, not to Pierrette Trichet.

Georges Clot agreed to introduce her to the tasting committee, where the gentlemen gave Pierette what she euphemistically described as a "cautious" welcome. At first, she was only

EAU-DE-VIE

The committee members have not eaten anything before the tasting, nor have they smoked, or used any type of fragrance. Each one "noses" and tastes and notes their findings, which are later compared with those of their colleagues. The Cellar Master then makes a decision; either accepting the eau-de-vie or asking the distiller to try again. Failing that, suggesting they look around for another customer. By April 1, as dictated by official regulations, the 00 cognac has become a 0, but is not yet marketable. After a trial by fire, it must now undergo a trial by wood.

Pierrette Trichet, Rémy Martin Cellar Master
from 2003 to 2014.

allowed to join them at the end of a session, so as not to "disturb the tasters." After a year's observation, she was allowed to participate in the whole session and taste the eaux-de-vie herself, and the Committee eventually admitted her—a woman, a scientist, a person not even born in Charente. Pierrette Trichet then entered the world of tasting, and tasting entered her world.

As Pierrette knew, a great cognac could only be identified by tasting, but she also knew that analysis could help to improve winegrowing practices. For Rémy Martin, it meant the guarantee of a supply that needed to increase in quality year after year to satisfy market demands. For the winegrowers, it meant the possibility of improving their eaux-de-vie sales, and sometimes of earning the bonus awarded to the best samples by the tasting committee.

What really made Pierrette Trichet happy was not discovering this or that mysterious molecule, but offering useful advice to a specific winegrower or distiller to improve their production. As a farmer's daughter herself, she knew how important it was to recognize the work of the land.

A positive outcome to the crisis entailed offering products of ever higher quality and opening up to new markets. One of those markets—China—would have a considerable influence on the future of Rémy Martin. At that time, the country was recording double-digit economic growth, and since 1992, a new economic wind had been blowing. Communist leader Deng Xiaoping officially authorized his compatriots to do business for their personal enrichment, which some people had already been doing for a decade. The new Chinese entrepreneurs were not only making money; they were also flaunting their success by liberally spending part of their earnings. The restaurants, nightclubs, and department stores that were springing up everywhere gave them plenty of opportunity to do so.

Few Western entrepreneurs believed in the Chinese awakening at that time. Bosses and bankers alike exercised the greatest caution, but Marc and François Hériard Dubreuil were in no doubt. For over ten years, they had been convinced that China—a country that had

EAU-DE-VIE

CHARENTE MEETS THE LIMOUSIN. The Charente wine trade developed because of the salt pans, as previously discussed. It is also the reason behind the alliance of eau-de-vie and Limousin oak. In the Middle Ages, the wagon drivers who came to pick up loads at the river port of Cognac were unwilling to travel empty. With no other goods to exchange for the salt, they loaded up with timber, cut from the forests covering their land. And thus ensured that Charente eau-de-vie could become cognac.

1985 advertisement for the Chinese market, with Larry Hagman,
who starred as J.R. Ewing in the TV series *Dallas*.

TO SAVOR AN OLD COGNAC, WHICH GOES VERY WELL WITH MANY LOCAL DISHES, IS TO FLAUNT ONE'S SUCCESS.

The Chinese are fond of cognac and often drink it with meals, like their traditional grain alcohol, *baijiu*. In Beijing and Shanghai, it can be drunk in a small glass in one shot, followed by a glass of water. But unlike *baijiu*, cognac is a social marker. To savor an old cognac, which goes very well with many local dishes, is to flaunt one's success, and as the idea is to stand out from the crowd, one might just as well choose Rémy Martin, the most prestigious brand. The greater one's success, the greater the cognac should be. Not a VSOP, therefore, but an XO. The Charente tradition became a symbol of Chinese modernity.

generated a quarter of the world's wealth until the eighteenth century—would eventually regain its status as one of the world's greatest powers. They had been waiting for this turnaround for ten years, and it had finally arrived. In this new game, Rémy Martin was not only one step ahead of its competitors; it also held a trump card. The company was already well established in China thanks to Dynasty Fine Wines, a joint venture set up by François Hériard Dubreuil in 1980 which, although not particularly profitable, turned out to be a wonderful door opener. Dynasty was the wine drunk by all the dignitaries of the Chinese Communist Party—the very people who could open doors in a country that was, admittedly, in the process of liberalization, but was still bound by bureaucracy.

A fast-growing Chinese market.

EAU-DE-VIE

Cognac is indeed the result of the blend between Charente eau-de-vie and Limousin oak. Officially, the casks can be made with Limousin oak or with oak from the Tronçais forest. Purists, however, are adamant. Tronçais oak, however splendid the tree, does not possess the characteristic tannins or porosity of the Limousin variety.

> **KNOWN BY ITS CENTAUR LOGO, THE BRAND GALLOPED FAR AHEAD OF ITS COMPETITORS, AND SALES INCREASED YEAR AFTER YEAR.**

While others were still doubting the reality of the country's economic opening, Rémy Martin literally created the cognac market in China in the early 1990s. Known by its centaur logo, the brand galloped far ahead of its competitors, and sales increased year after year. On their frequent visits to China, François and Marc Hériard Dubreuil were given a VIP welcome and spared the bother of border-crossing formalities. On those surreal occasions, the brothers could savor the pleasure of having been right before everyone else.

However, having got it right was no protection against the vagaries of fate. What became known as the Asian crisis began in the summer of 1997 in Thailand, whose currency and stock market plummeted. By a domino effect, the crisis spread to Southeast Asia, Taiwan, South Korea, and even Hong Kong, as that region was also a big consumer of cognac. All brands combined, sales to Asia fell by a third, and in Hong Kong, they dropped by half. In 1998, the Chinese market, initially thought to have avoided the disaster, shrank in turn. Global growth came to a standstill, and the Cognac region was hard hit. The shock was all the more brutal because Southeast Asia had a far greater love of old cognacs than the United States. To anticipate demand, large stocks of eau-de-vie had to be built up several years in advance, which was possible as long as sales kept growing, but when the economic winds turned, the consequences were multiplied. The Cognac vineyards could produce a million hectoliters of pure alcohol per year, but the market could absorb barely half of that. The cognac houses were overflowing with stocks, their debts increased, and prices collapsed.

An expert Cellar Master must be as demanding about the wood for his cask as he is about the eaux-de-vie the casks will contain; he must be sure that they work together. Rémy Martin primarily chooses Pedunculate Oak from the Limousin region, whose large open grain is conducive to developing the aromatic intensity of the Champagne eaux-de-vie.

EAU-DE-VIE

A vineyard adaptation plan was signed in July 1997, providing for the uprooting of thousands of acres of vines, but the results would take a few years to show. The winegrowers, some of whom were on the verge of bankruptcy, gave vent to their anger and blocked the town of Cognac for several days. Many of them were desperate, including the suppliers of Rémy Martin, which had also been obliged to reduce its purchases. Multi-year contracts once again helped to cushion the blow, but the headwinds were too strong. The young Rémy Cointreau group—which had taken on a lot of debt to expand and to finance its distribution network and fifty or so subsidiaries—was not strong enough to withstand this economic downturn. Marc Hériard Dubreuil would later admit that he and his brother, their eyes riveted on China, had been slow to appreciate the financial risk to the group. In 1997, it recorded losses of over six hundred million francs, almost a hundred million euros. The situation was critical: the very survival of the group was at stake, and with it, the future of Rémy Martin cognac.

> THE SITUATION WAS CRITICAL: THE VERY SURVIVAL OF THE GROUP WAS AT STAKE, AND WITH IT, THE FUTURE OF RÉMY MARTIN COGNAC.

1998 Dominique Hériard Dubreuil, who was appointed president of Rémy Cointreau at the beginning of 1998, and her brothers, who were still in charge of its general management, made a series of drastic decisions. As the group was in dire need of cash, it would sell off some of its activities, including two Champagne houses: De Venoge, acquired less than three years earlier, and Krug. Both were good businesses and were sold reluctantly, but their sale helped to stabilize the group's accounts. In addition, the group decided to break away from its global distribution network, which the brand portfolio could not support. More precisely, it decided to share it with two other players in the liquor industry: the Scottish group Highland Distillers, and the American group Jim Beam—soon joined by the Swedish group Vin & Spirit—forming a global distribution network. However, at the last moment, Rémy Cointreau announced its intention to keep its American activities in-house. Having weighed the pros and cons at length, François and Marc Hériard Dubreuil made a late-night decision to take this gamble, to the great displeasure of their future partners. The agreement was signed the next day, and a joint network called Maxxium was created, but Rémy Cointreau kept its subsidiary in the United States. A few years later, when the American market took off again, the brothers could congratulate themselves for having made that decision. For the time being,

EAU-DE-VIE

From a 150-year-old oak tree, a cooper can cut just enough wood for two or three 350-liter casks, the standard size at Rémy Martin. The tree is felled during the winter when the sap is not running, and cut into squared logs. Each log is split into four quarters, from which staves are split, after the bark and core have been removed. The wood is never saw-cut, because the flavor of the wood is lost when the grain is cut.

Inaugurated in 1892, the Francis cellar is a remarkable example of a cathedral cellar.

they were acting on intuition, convinced that Rémy Martin's historic American subsidiary was so deeply rooted in the company's history that it could not be separated from it.

The crisis had been overcome, and the group then had to learn from its past mistakes and move forward. Dominique Hériard Dubreuil was in charge of stabilizing and rebuilding the group, and relaunching Rémy Martin. Her two brothers were piloting another project: that of the family holding company, Andromède. Its single objective was to create a small conglomerate whose financial base would be sufficient to protect Rémy Cointreau from future crises, because there was no doubt about it, the market would face other crises in the future.

COCKTAILS WERE COMING BACK INTO FASHION.

This was the beginning of a period of multiple initiatives to expand the brand portfolio, create new products, and propose new consumption methods. One of the avenues explored was the production of Charentais wine. On the family Grollet Estate, some fifty acres (twenty hectares) of vines had been converted at the initiative of André Hériard Dubreuil in the 1990s, with the idea of testing an alternative outlet that would be less cyclical than cognac. The partner winegrowers were invited to take part in the venture, and 350 of them agreed to experiment on part of the estate with the production of a wine other than that destined for cognac. The first bottles of red wine could then be marketed. Unfortunately, they arrived on the market at a bad time: French wine production was facing a decline in domestic consumption, along with competition from other exporting countries. Despite the recognized quality of the new Charentais wine and the efforts made to promote it, their early hopes were dashed. Little by little, the vineyards were returned to their former purpose: the production of cognac.

Experimentation in other areas was more fruitful. Cocktails were coming back into fashion, and there was a growing market for premixes—ready-to-drink mixes of alcoholic and non-alcoholic drinks. Rémy Martin added some bold innovations to its traditional products: Rémy Platinum, then Rémy Silver, a mix of cognac and vodka. Then came Rémy Red, a combination of Fine Champagne cognac and red fruit, with strawberry-kiwi-orange and grape-blueberry-apple versions following shortly after. This creative fever spread beyond cognac; the group also marketed Mount Gay rums with Madagascan vanilla or Mexican mango flavors. Purists may have found these innovations surprising or even upsetting, but

The staves are stored outside, where they are seasoned for three to four years in the timber yard. This drying period can be accelerated by regularly spraying the wood with water; this shortens it by one year, at most. Like the oak from which they were cut, staves require time before all the humidity and bitterness of its tannins have been removed.

Mixology offers a multitude of creative options for tasting cognac. Cédric Bouteiller, Rémy Martin's expert, preparing a Sidecar, an Old Fashioned and a Rémy Ginger.

they were not the target customers. The new products corresponded to the needs of a new era eager for gaiety and glamor.

> DOMINIQUE HÉRIARD DUBREUIL WAS WILLING TO ENVISAGE ALL KINDS OF EXPERIMENTATION ON ONE CONDITION: THAT THE VALUES OF THE COGNAC HOUSE AND ITS FLAGSHIP PRODUCTS SHOULD REMAIN INTACT.

Sticklers for tradition had no cause for concern: the new style of marketing remained under control, Dominique Hériard Dubreuil made sure of that. She was willing to envisage all kinds of experimentation on one condition: that the values of the cognac house and its flagship products should remain intact. Some things cannot be compromised on—not because of a hankering for the past, but on the contrary, because they ensure the future of the brand. Before long, the American photographer David LaChapelle would dress up a bottle of VSOP with a scantily clad, hip-wiggling dancer, but its contents would always be the VSOP Fine Champagne cognac beloved of André Renaud and André Hériard Dubreuil.

2000

The group soon became profitable again, with cognac not its bestseller but its main source of profit. The market, more volatile than that of eau-de-vie, took off again from the early 2000s, and the winegrowers regained hope. Interest in cognac revived in the United States, and Rémy Cointreau Americas—the subsidiary the group had decided to keep at the last minute—was doing well. For the most part, the African-American community was behind this renewed interest, for reasons dating back to the First World War, when tens of thousands of Black American soldiers landed in France to help in the fight against Germany. Having come to fight for democracy, they were met with tolerance, whereas they were still victims of racial segregation back home, and their own army confined them to supply roles. Black Americans not only helped the Allies win the war; they also introduced jazz to France, where it had previously been known only to a few—and they took cognac back home as a souvenir.

> IT SPREAD TO ALL THE TRENDY NIGHT SPOTS OF A MULTICULTURAL, JOYFUL, AND LAID-BACK AMERICA, CONTRIBUTING TO THE STRONG GROWTH OF THE MARKET IN THE 2000S.

EAU-DE-VIE

After this long wait, during which the master cooper closely monitors the aging of the wood, the staves are then trimmed and made up into sets, each set corresponding to one cask. The staves are fashioned so that they fit together perfectly when the cask is assembled. The cooper assembles the staves in the form of an inverted "rose," with the hooped end uppermost, and puts it over a wood fire. The staves are simultaneously heated and moistened to soften the fibers of the wood, releasing a tantalizing smell of vanilla and boiling sugar in the process.

THE SPIRIT OF COGNAC

Rémy Martin is a longstanding supplier of the Cannes Film Festival.
Since 2010, jury members have signed the year's limited edition decanters.

The combination of African-American music and Charente eau-de-vie has continued ever since, and has even grown stronger. After jazz, soul and hip-hop embraced cognac in turn. In the late 1990s, rap even made it a symbol of successful Black Americans. In contrast to whisky, the liquor of white America, cognac was adopted by the Black American community, and soon by the Asian and Hispanic communities too. From there, it spread to all the trendy night spots of a multicultural, joyful, and laid-back America, contributing to the strong growth of the market in the 2000s.

> COGNAC WAS AN ESSENTIAL INGREDIENT IN THE COCKTAILS THAT WERE BECOMING FASHIONABLE ON THE NEW YORK NIGHTLIFE SCENE.

For Rémy Martin, there were two aspects to this revival. On the one hand, cognac was an essential ingredient in the cocktails that were becoming fashionable on the New York nightlife scene—and relatively young cognacs were ideal for that purpose. And on the other hand, as rappers loved to flaunt their wealth, they helped to build an awareness and appreciation of more high-end products, such as the 1738 Accord Royal, created by Georges Clot and introduced on the market at the hefty price of fifty-five dollars a bottle. It was first launched in Japan in 1997, a very bad year for new products, and it did not prosper. It was, however, a great success in the United States, with its generously shaped bottle, along the lines of a bottle of bourbon. Older cognacs also conquered a new market and new venues very different from the hushed, conservative lounges where they were usually found. The star rapper Jay-Z (who had

This operation is extremely delicate. The wood must be softened but not charred. The cooper knows by touch when the wood is ready to give, telling him when to tighten the staves with a winch. The staves are tightened gradually to form the curved shape, and the winch cables are then replaced with a second iron hoop.

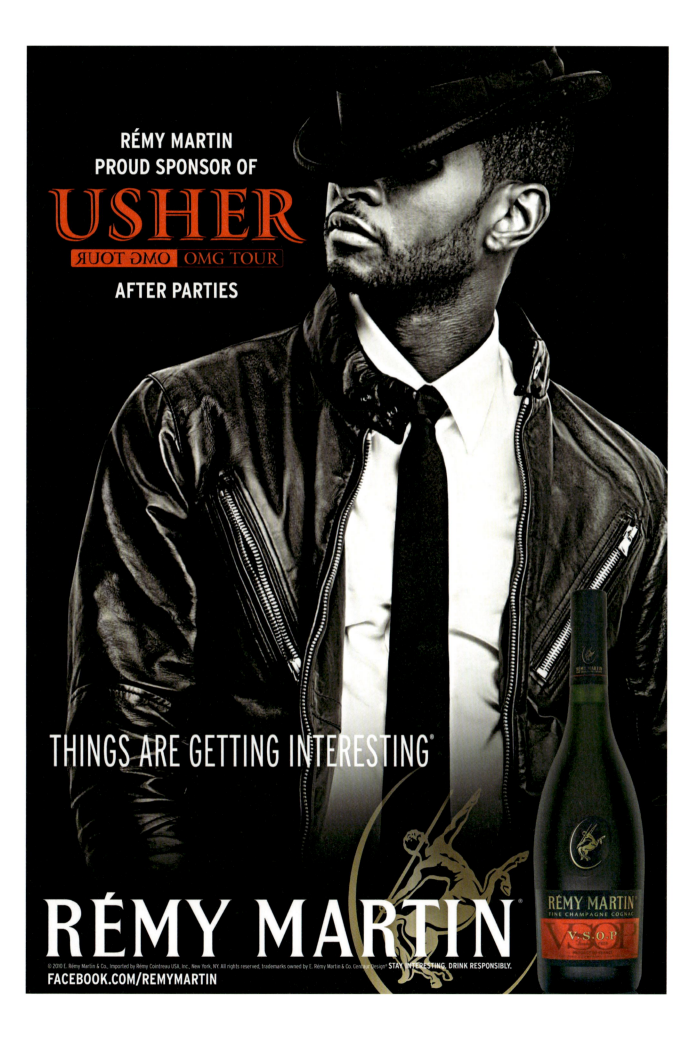

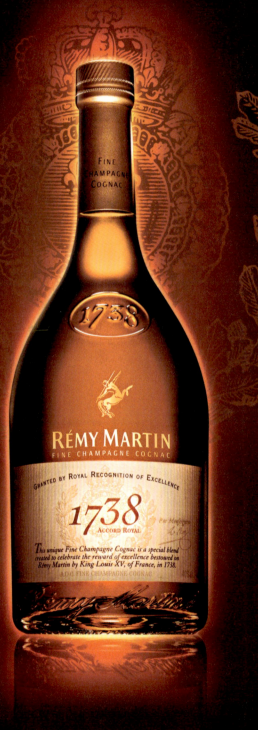

already mentioned "Rémy" in "Can't Knock the Hustle"), opened a "Rémy Lounge" at his iconic 40/40 Club in New York, where, for a few hundred dollars, you could buy a taste of Louis XIII Diamant with its diamond-encrusted stopper.

Although America was largely responsible for the revival of the cognac market in the early twenty-first century, Asia was not outdone. The shock of 1998 was quickly overcome, especially in China, and market demand for cognac—mainly quality cognac—was increasing. The days when the brand was reserved for officials were long gone. Now, the "man-headed horse" cognac, as it is known there, was available to anyone affected by the winds of liberalism, not only in Beijing or Shanghai, but also in the south of the country, in Xiamen or Guangzhou. The Club cognac was snapped up, XO became a reference, and specific products such as the 1898 Coupe Fine Champagne were in great demand. For several years, sales in China grew by double digits, driven by trendy bars and restaurants, and dance and karaoke clubs.

It would be simplistic to see this early-2000s trend simply as a boom in creative marketing designed to conquer new markets. While American and Chinese nightlife was glittering, and the most outlandish cocktails were being mixed in Singapore and Vietnam, and the wildest parties held in London, Berlin, and Moscow, the people in charge back in Cognac and Paris were keeping their feet firmly on the ground. With a return to growth and profits, two paths lay ahead for the Rémy Cointreau group.

WHILE AMERICAN AND CHINESE NIGHTLIFE WAS GLITTERING, THE PEOPLE IN CHARGE BACK IN COGNAC WERE KEEPING THEIR FEET FIRMLY ON THE GROUND.

The ends of the cask are assembled with wooden pends; no nails or glue. They are then sealed with rushes cut in the summer from the banks of the Charente river. The cask is then ready to receive its permanent hoops. In a strange duel with his hammer, the cooper then proceeds with an operation, testing the cask, which reverberates like a drum. If the sound is right, the cask is good, meaning that the wood is properly seasoned and the cask assembled correctly. All that remains is to flush the cask through with boiling water, to scald the inside, and verify that it is watertight.

EAU-DE-VIE

Louis XIII took over the world's capitals in a 2021 campaign for social media; here, London.

The first was to pursue a multi-directional expansion strategy in order to hold their own in the fierce battle between the global giants of wine and liquor distribution. Present from Argentina to Zimbabwe, specializing in cognac but also active in the markets for wine, champagne, whisky, vodka, gin, and brandy, the group could legitimately consider this strategy which, if successful, would spare them from getting caught up again in the turbulence of the cognac market. But it was not without risks. The desire to gain market shares at any cost entailed the risk of losing one's soul through over-diversification. That would represent a departure from the initial mission of the cognac house and the fundamental choices of Paul-Émile Rémy Martin, André Renaud, and André Hériard Dubreuil. It would create a gap between Rémy Martin and all the winegrowers who kept the brand alive, when it had always drawn its strength from their closeness.

> **RÉMY MARTIN COGNAC ONLY MADE SENSE BECAUSE IT ORIGINATED IN THE VINEYARDS OF GRANDE AND PETITE CHAMPAGNE, AGED MOSTLY IN COARSE-GRAINED FRENCH OAK BARRELS FROM THE LIMOUSIN REGION.**

2004 The second path was the obvious choice: the future lay in the quest for value rather than volume. It was preferable to remain a modestly sized but profitable group in line with its values, rather than seek growth at all costs. This value strategy, which was confirmed in 2004 and was always deeply rooted in the company's history, would lead the group to divest itself of certain brands in 2005 in order to focus on the so-called "premium" brands with strong potential. The following year, Rémy Cointreau announced its intention to leave the Maxxium network, whose partners had changed and whose objectives no longer matched its own.

The trial and error of the turn of the century was well and truly over, the course was clearly set, and it was the responsibility of Jean-Marie Laborde, the group's CEO since 2004, to stay on that course. The future did not lie in standardized liquors that would dominate the global market, but in a range of more or less complex products associated with particular terroirs, each telling its own specific story. This was not just an objective; it was the heart and soul of the company. Rémy Martin cognac only made sense because it originated in the vineyards of Grande and Petite Champagne, aged mostly in coarse-grained French oak barrels from the Limousin region, and then came into its own in the shade of the Merpins cellars, under the watchful eye of Pierrette Trichet, who took

THE CASK'S CHARACTER. The finished cask, duly signed by the cooper, is slightly permeable to air and ready for the long aging process, during which it will impart its tannins and some of its aromatic characteristics to the cognac. Like any other living thing, its youth will be impetuous, before it grows wiser with the passing years. A cask is considered "new" for its first five years, when it is used for young eaux-de-vie.

over from Georges Clot in 2003. She had been the obvious choice to succeed him. Ignoring any misogynistic comments, Dominique Hériard Dubreuil chose Pierrette Trichet for her skills and her ability to continue the work begun years before: to constantly improve the quality of Rémy Martin cognacs.

The Louis XIII cognac, a gem among gems, would set the standard for this quest for excellence. There was no need to invent a new product, it already existed, and any attempt to change it would be a grave mistake. It just needed to be elevated above cognac, given the place it deserved in the world of luxury rather than that of liquors. In 2003, looking for someone with a fresh perspective to steer the project, Dominique Hériard Dubreuil chose Augustin Depardon, then in charge of the group's young and trendy liquors. The first objective she set him was perfectly clear: "Augustin, with Louis XIII we have an excellent market ahead of us. We have to raise our prices!"

> **THE LOUIS XIII COGNAC JUST NEEDED TO BE ELEVATED ABOVE COGNAC, GIVEN THE PLACE IT DESERVED IN THE WORLD OF LUXURY RATHER THAN THAT OF LIQUORS.**

Having chaired the Comité Colbert, an institution representing French luxury houses, from 1994 to 1998, she knew what she was talking about. In the world of luxury, price is only a problem if it is too low. Louis XIII—an exceptional cognac that takes more than a lifetime to produce, a complex blend of eaux-de-vie coming exclusively from the Grande Champagne cru, the fruit of the work of several generations of Cellar Masters—was worth far more than the 600 euros that each decanter was sold for. Dominique Hériard Dubreuil stuck to her guns on this matter, and made it one of her priorities when she arrived in Cognac. When she overheard someone in the office organizing a promotional campaign on Louis XIII, she reacted immediately: the next day, a memo was circulated to all the staff, formally prohibiting such practices for that product. Since that day, no Louis XIII decanters have ever been discounted. The king of cognacs should never be sold for less than its worth.

It takes legitimacy and know-how—guarantees of perfection—to gain acceptance into the world of luxury. In that respect, Louis XIII was every bit as good as haute couture or high jewelry pieces. And the fact that it had a history was an added advantage. The history of Louis XIII cognac began in 1874 with Paul-Émile Rémy Martin, and continued at the Paris Exposition of 1900, on the legendary Orient

The first time, the eau-de-vie spends only a few months in the new cask to avoid absorbing too much tannin and becoming bitter with its aromas smothered. The second time, the cognac can be left in the cask for up to two years; and the third time, longer still. When the cask is filled for the fourth time it is said to be "seasoned," and has reached the age of reason. Cognac can be left in this cask for several years. A cask is considered fully mature after ten years, and can remain in use in the cellars for several more decades.

The Porte des Lions, the entrance to the Grollet Estate.

> IT TAKES LEGITIMACY AND KNOW-HOW—GUARANTEES OF PERFECTION—TO GAIN ACCEPTANCE INTO THE WORLD OF LUXURY.

Express in the late 1920s, on the maiden voyage of the SS Normandie ocean liner in 1935, and later, aboard the supersonic Concorde. Its history often intersected with major world events, and crossed paths with distinguished figures such as Sir Winston Churchill and President Kennedy.

2006 However, it is one thing to enter the world of luxury, and quite another to stay there. The latter requires constant creativity. Rémy Martin provided a dazzling example in 2006 with the creation of Black Pearl, a limited-edition cognac aged in an exceptional hundred-year-old *tierçon* oak barrel, one of the oldest in the storehouses. Such a cognac naturally required an exceptional decanter. Augustin Depardon nurtured the idea with his partners from the prestigious Baccarat crystal factory.

One day, at a meeting, he noticed a beautiful black lamp designed by Philippe Starck—a small object with metallic reflections oscillating between silver and black, chrome and steel blue. Struck by a sudden intuition, he asked, "Could we imagine a Louis XIII decanter with the same changing reflections, opaque or translucent according to the angle of the light?" "Impossible," came the Baccarat designers' swift reply. "What can be done with this small, streamlined lamp with its smooth shade could never be achieved with a decanter as complex as that of Louis XIII. Technically, it's inconceivable!"

Two months later, a member of the Baccarat team showed up at Augustin Depardon's office. With a twinkle in her eye, she placed a Louis XIII decanter with mysterious metallic reflections on his desk. What had been considered impossible had been achieved, Baccarat had taken on the challenge, and the exceptional *tierçon* barrel cognac now had a suitably exceptional decanter. Each Black Pearl decanter was priced at between six and seven thousand euros—a price that, even at Rémy Martin, many people considered astronomical.

Sir Winston Churchill was an aficionado of Louis XIII cognac.

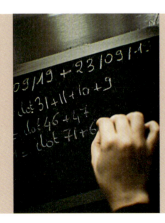

When the eau-de-vie is first placed in the casks, it is colorless. The aging process is monitored constantly by the Cellar Master. Their most valued ally is time itself. The eau-de-vie's rating improves year by year: it is numbered 2 after two years and can been sold as a Three Star or VS. After four years, it can claim VSOP status, after six it has become a Napoleon, and by ten, an XO or an Extra. But these are only legal obligations.

The Louis XIII Black Pearl decanter with metallic reflections is a technical feat achieved by the master glassmakers of Baccarat.

The company offered 786 decanters for sale, the total contents of the single *tierçon* barrel—but it received requests for 4,000 decanters, far exceeding its wildest expectations.

WHAT MATTERED MOST WAS THAT AN ENCOUNTER WITH LOUIS XIII SHOULD BE AN UNFORGETTABLE EXPERIENCE.

After the success of Black Pearl, other creations followed over the years. An event that particularly marked Pierrette Trichet was the party held in Guilin, China, for the 2009 launch of Louis XIII Rare Cask 43,8, in a superb decor representing terraced rice fields. Other people were mightily impressed by the launch of the second edition— Louis XIII Rare Cask 42,6—a few years later, in a magical atmosphere in the presence of the Maharana of Udaipur. Whether in China, in India, or in the darkness of the cellars on the Grollet Estate, what mattered most was that an encounter with Louis XIII should be an unforgettable experience. Little by little, Louis XIII established itself as a luxury brand on par with the greatest, proud of its winegrowing roots and its link to Grande Champagne, that tiny piece of planet Earth where a facet of human genius shines brighter than anywhere else.

The 2000s marked the beginning of this new Louis XIII saga, and bore the seeds of success for the following decade. Louis XIII would carry the whole cognac house—indeed, the whole Rémy Cointreau group—in its wake into a new world where craftsmanship was elevated to the rank of a major art. The "value strategy" devised by Dominique, François, and Marc Hériard Dubreuil at the beginning of the century—which went against contemporary trends and provoked snide comments from the other liquor groups and a certain apprehension among the company's sales staff—had proved to be a winner. "It was obvious," drily remarked Dominique Hériard Dubreuil years later.

LOUIS XIII ESTABLISHED ITSELF AS A LUXURY BRAND ON PAR WITH THE GREATEST, PROUD OF ITS WINEGROWING ROOTS AND ITS LINK TO GRANDE CHAMPAGNE.

A PRECIOUS CELLAR. In his cellar with nothing but cognac and more cognac, where time stands still, the Cellar Master prepares his masterpieces. The walls of local stone and the bare, chalky earthen floor maintain a nearly constant temperature, nursing the slow maturation of the cognac. Inside the cask the cognac breathes, absorbing oxygen from the air and evaporating through the porous staves. Some of the cognac is lost each year, blackening the walls and roof of the cellar as the "angels' share," *la part des anges*, wafts away. This mysterious tithe contributes much to the quality of the cognac.

In 2023, the third edition of the Louis XIII Rare Cask (42,1) was unveiled in Venice.

Another important fact was that cognac, the fruit of the earth and of human labor, should exhaust neither the earth nor human beings. It was no coincidence that the company's commitment to sustainable development was concomitant with the value strategy introduced in the early 2000s. Excellence in a product of the earth cannot be achieved by destroying the terroir in which it grows—and the production of a century-old eau-de-vie requires a lot of forward planning. In late 2002, Dominique Hériard Dubreuil entrusted Christian Lafage, Head of Quality for the group in Cognac, with the task of steering what she considered an essential project. At that time, few people were interested in setting out a corporate sustainability approach, but Christian Lafage was an exception. A sustainable development department was created in 2003, and the same year, the group decided to sign the United Nations Global Compact, the first international agreement encouraging social and environmental responsibility. This was not mere posturing: signatories of the charter must assess their progress year by year, and be veritable ambassadors for the respect of human rights and the environment.

Rémy Martin could not commit to this charter alone; it needed its historic partners, the winegrowers. The stakes were huge for them too, as the Charente vineyards were beginning to feel the effects of climate change. The grapes were being harvested earlier and earlier, and drought years and hailstorms were becoming increasingly frequent. Moreover, as the vines were emerging from dormancy earlier in the year, they ran a greater risk of falling victim to a late frost. While the world was struggling to accept the reality of these changes, the winegrowers were already suffering the consequences.

How, despite such hazards, could it be ensured that Grande and Petite Champagne vineyards would continue to produce the same exceptional eaux-de-vie in the decades to come? Rémy Martin did not commit to this project as an ordering party—a merchant imposing new conditions on suppliers—but as one winemaker among others. Just as the Grollet Estate had made it possible to test the production of red wine, the Domaines Rémy Martin would become the real-life field of experimentation of more environmentally friendly production methods. The future of Rémy Martin cognac, be it VSOP or Louis XIII, was being played out in the gray soil of the Champagne vineyards, far from the bars and luxury hotels where it is enjoyed. A future that depended on respect for the land, its forests, hedges, and natural reservoirs; on the preparation of the soils and the planting of the vineyards; on the pruning of the vines and their protection against disease; on the management of waste and wastewater; and on distillation, too. Everything needed to be reviewed.

The cognac is at 70 degrees of alcohol at the start of the aging process, and loses between 2 to 3 percent each year as it gradually reaches the 40 degree of alcohol legal minimum. Below this it is no longer entitled to its appellation. If the cognac is bottled before it reaches this level, it must be "cut" with distilled water. This is not necessary if it is aged for many years. It will then have consumed much more of the original eau-de-vie, while acquiring a beautiful reddish-brown color from its long stay in the cask.

Rémy Martin's first sustainable viticulture charter was adopted in 2004. Three years later, the Rémy Martin estates obtained the official "sustainable viticulture" certification, guaranteeing constant attention to the environment, the control of health risks, and, more generally, health and safety at work. The objective was not to showcase a model vineyard, but to experiment with practices that each winegrower could then adopt.

The Rémy Martin estates were becoming a reference by proving that new practices were possible and were both technically and economically viable.

2007 At that time, in August 2007, a young enologist joined the company. His name was Baptiste Loiseau, and he was not yet twenty-seven years old. Pierrette Trichet recruited him to assist her with the winegrowers, to be "her eyes and voice." Although he was young, he was not a total novice as he had previously worked for the *chambre d'agriculture* farm bureau on the first guide to "sustainable viticulture" for the winegrowers in the Cognac appellation area. He had grown up in the village of Genté, and had attended the same school as Nicolas Hériard Dubreuil, one of François's sons, but he only knew the company by reputation—a reputation that prompted him, when he heard that they were looking for a consulting engineer, to try his luck and send his resume.

BAPTISTE LOISEAU THREW HIMSELF WHOLEHEARTEDLY INTO THE JOB.

Baptiste Loiseau's mission was to work with the winegrowers, to help them make the best possible wine while respecting the land from which it comes. He threw himself wholeheartedly into the job, spending one day out in the vineyards, the next in the basement of the laboratory, the day after that in the distillery. With enthusiasm and curiosity, he learned, listened, explained, and experimented under Pierrette Trichet's benevolent eye. It all paid off, as the quality of the eaux-de-vie improved year by year, which was good news for Rémy Martin, as it strengthened its strategy of moving upmarket. Fewer and

THE CELLAR MASTER. The cellar, with its rows of casks protected from bugs by the many spiders and their webs, is a silent world of odours, where time passes at a pace unlike anywhere else. The Cellar Master is not a technician, but an artist, who has learned to assess each blend after many long years of initiation. In the larger cognac houses, science has now come to the aid of the Cellar Master. Sophisticated analytical methods are used to establish the relationship between the properties of a cognac and its composition.

THE SPIRIT OF COGNAC

Baptiste Loiseau, Cellar Master since 2014.

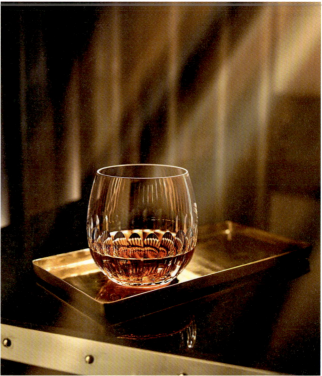

Rémy Martin cognacs can be enjoyed as cocktails, but also neat or on the rocks.

fewer of the winegrowers' batches were rejected, so they also reaped the benefits. Pierrette Trichet had a memorable experience the day before the Christmas vacation, when she was validating the tasting notes. "Great!" she suddenly exclaimed when she saw the name of a winegrower whose sample had been rejected at the previous tasting.

This time, the tasting panel had awarded the sample a 10 percent bonus, the highest possible rating. Without a second thought, Pierrette Trichet departed from the rule of never giving the results by phone, and called the winegrower. It was almost 8 p.m. when he picked up the phone and recognized the Cellar Master's voice. After a moment's fraught silence, he whispered, "What's happened? Has my sample been rejected again?" "On the contrary, it's been awarded 10 percent!" came the reply. At the other end of the line, the winegrower was jubilant, but perhaps less so than Pierrette Trichet, who was never as happy as when she felt she had helped a winegrower to produce what might be, in several decades, an eau-de-vie that would go into the blend of a Louis XIII.

> ALTHOUGH THE GROWTH OF THE GROUP COULD HAVE WEAKENED THE RELATIONSHIP BETWEEN RÉMY MARTIN AND THE WINEGROWERS, IT WAS ACTUALLY STRENGTHENED IN MANY RESPECTS.

A winegrower signing a partnership agreement.

Although the growth of the Rémy Cointreau group could have weakened the relationship between Rémy Martin and the winegrowers, it was actually strengthened in many respects. In addition to cultivation practices, this was confirmed in the financial field in 2005, with the unprecedented consolidation of the founding pact of 1965. That year, a new cooperative called "Alliance Fine Champagne," created from the merger of the historic cooperative Champaco and the distillers' cooperative Prochacoop, acquired a stake in the capital of the Rémy Cointreau group.

"We know each other well enough to be able to speak frankly," said François and Marc Hériard Dubreuil. "Look around you; one by one the cognac houses are passing into the hands of large financial groups. None of us

As each cask has a digital ID, the Cellar Master knows the quality and location of each batch. This helps them assess the specific characteristics of each blend created by their predecessors. Although this can lighten the workload, science cannot rival a Cellar Master for determining a blend, no more than it can compose the most captivating symphonies or the most moving poems.

want to take that path. You have some money set aside in your cooperative. If you invest it in Rémy Martin, it will be good for us, but it will be good for you too."

FROM SIMPLE DELIVERERS, THEN PARTNER WINEGROWERS, THEY WENT ON TO BECOME ASSOCIATE PARTNERS. THE FUTURE WOULD SHOW THAT THEIR INVESTMENT WAS EXTREMELY PROFITABLE.

At the instigation of Bernard Guionnet—a key figure in regional winegrowers' trade unions, and president of Champaco, then of Alliance Fine Champagne, from 1994 until his death in 2011—the cooperative members accepted the proposal. In an unprecedented operation, they invested some of their reserve funds in the group's development, and in exchange were paid dividends in addition to their remuneration. From simple deliverers, then partner winegrowers, they went on to become associate partners. The future would show that their investment was extremely profitable. In addition, it proved that the relationship of trust was still strong, even if it took different forms from one generation to the next.

2010 The 2000s allowed the winegrowers to resurface after a decade of crisis, but also to reinvent their relationship with the company. After some initial trial and error, the group managed to find its way. The following decade saw a return to serenity. André and Anne-Marie Hériard Dubreuil's children were still in charge of the group. In 2012, Dominique handed over the presidency to her brother François, who in turn passed it on to his brother Marc in 2017. Whoever was president, key decisions continued to be made together, in consultation with the CEO Jean-Marie Laborde, within what among themselves they called the "G4." However, they were all aware that they had to think about their succession. Was the new generation—that of their children—interested in taking over? If so, it was time to prepare.

The Hériard Dubreuils' favorite place for a family reunion was Charente, but the twelve grandchildren of Anne-Marie and André Hériard Dubreuil (who died in 2002) were scattered all over the world, so this time they decided to meet at the Charles de Gaulle airport in Paris, one weekend in 2008 when some of them were in transit between flights. "That day, very clearly, my uncles and my mother asked us if we were interested in the succession," Marie-Amélie de Leusse, Dominique Hériard Dubreuil's daughter, said later. "At

The cognac may need to take another tack during the aging process. After tasting it, the Cellar Master may have the cognac transferred to another cask, from a new one to a "seasoned" one, or from a seasoned cask to a very old one. Or he may move the cognac to another cellar. In a humid cellar, the eau-de-vie loses its alcohol more rapidly and can become flat. In a dry cellar, the angels may be overly greedy: the liquid evaporates faster, and the eau-de-vie can harden. In some cases, the cognac may even spend some time in the loft, in an entirely different environment, as in the past, when casks undertook long voyages across the seas.

Winegrower partners of the Alliance Fine Champagne around Christophe Forget, its president, in 2019.

the very least, we would have to prepare to become good shareholders; and perhaps to take on operational responsibilities within the group."

In principle, they all agreed that the group should remain a family concern, but as they were all involved in their own professional activities, they needed time to think before committing to anything—at the risk of testing the patience of their elders. Nicolas Hériard Dubreuil, one of François's sons, was the first to take the plunge after a decisive lunch with his father and uncle, during which they told him that the time for reflection was over. As soon as he had finished his *sole meunière* and given them a positive answer, he made an appointment with the CEO, who sent him to the United States to experience the reality of the markets for himself. Dorothée Hériard Dubreuil, Marc's daughter-in-law, and Marie-Amélie de Leusse followed closely behind. In 2010, the former began working in sales in the French joint venture Lixir; the latter as a financial controller, first in Europe and then in Singapore. The following year, François's daughter Caroline Bois and Marc's daughter Laure Hériard Dubreuil joined the group's board of directors. They were later joined by their cousin Élie, Michel Hériard Dubreuil's son.

Blending is the ultimate privilege of the Cellar Master. Each blend is planned carefully ahead of time, even anticipating the aging process for his successors, so as to combine aromas and flavors that will remain complementary throughout the life of the cognac. They know that the development of an eau-de-vie is not linear. It consists of successive periods of lethargy, interspersed with abrupt changes that vary according to the blending process, the casks, and the environment in which they are stored.

In Paris, New York, and Singapore, both inside and outside the group, the younger generation went through the learning process and found their feet. They invented a new form of corporate governance, as twenty-four people—including the spouses, referred to in the family jargon as "added values"—cannot run a group the way four people can. They were all aware of the responsibilities inherent in belonging to this wealthy family, in particular that they would need to stay the course for the long haul. Their parents were passing on a legacy; they would do the same. But Nicolas Hériard Dubreuil did not see the previous generations' success as a burden. On the contrary. When asked the question, he said, "I see it the other way around. I feel I'm carried on the shoulders of the previous generations."

> **THE YOUNGER GENERATION WENT THROUGH THE LEARNING PROCESS AND FOUND THEIR FEET.**

Interestingly, in the dim cellars, Pierrette Trichet said more or less the same thing. When asked whether the responsibility of taking over from André Giraud and Georges Clot weighed heavily on her, she answered unhesitatingly, "When you find yourself alone in front of the blends that have to be made, you unconsciously allow the past Cellar Masters to guide you. They are present all around you. It's important to believe that!"

And on the subject of transmission: Pierrette Trichet was preparing to hand over the cellar keys to Baptiste Loiseau, the young man she had recruited a few years earlier to be her "eyes and voice" with the winegrowers. At the end of 2010, she told him she was looking for an assistant who could succeed her in a few years' time. "I'm telling you," she explained, "because I think you have the potential for the position." "Do you really think so?" he asked. "I don't think so, I know so!" she replied.

Marie-Amélie de Leusse, president of the Rémy Cointreau group and the House of Rémy Martin since 2022.

COGNAC

Each year, cognac houses take stock of the blends that have reached the desired maturity, when the strength of the wood fully matches that of the eau-de-vie, with neither dominating the other. A last tasting takes place prior to the final blending process. The Cellar Master first examines the color. He then uses his nose to assess the bouquet, the balance and the essential characteristics. He takes a little in his mouth, to determine its body and mellowness. His senses are awakened one by one as the ritual unfolds. Unconsciously, he closes his eyes as he inhales, all in silence. This is the moment when the Cellar Master decides what will be used in the final blend.

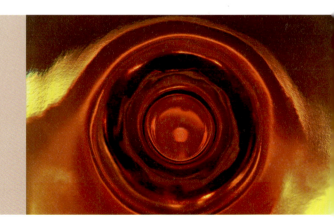

THE SPIRIT OF COGNAC

Cellar Masters: transmission of passion and savoir faire.

2014 Pierrette Trichet spent her days assessing the potential of young eaux-de-vie, so it was only natural for her to detect that of a young colleague. Week after week, she had observed Baptiste's progress, given him the opportunity to reveal his tasting skills, and witnessed his human qualities and storytelling talents. She had developed a genuine friendship with this young man who could have been her son, but in addition, she felt sure that he would not let her down. Baptiste Loiseau soon accepted the job, but he still needed the approval of Dominique Hériard Dubreuil. The latter's answer reflects the complicity between the two women. "I trust Pierrette," she said, "and I can see that she is confident. That's good enough for me." Baptiste Loiseau was appointed Cellar Master in April 2014, in the family home Le Grollet, on the eve of a memorable transition tour with Pierrette Trichet.

centuries-old company, renowned for its outstanding eaux-de-vie and with a worldwide turnover of over five hundred million euros, had entrusted the key to its treasure store to a young man in his thirties, and made him the guarantor of ancestral practices. But perhaps that is the true spirit of cognac—a spirit that Dominique Hériard Dubreuil has defended all her life: an unfailing trust in the future and in the men and women who have made, are making, and will continue to make cognac.

AN UNFAILING TRUST IN THE FUTURE AND IN THE MEN AND WOMEN WHO HAVE MADE, ARE MAKING, AND WILL CONTINUE TO MAKE COGNAC.

When described as above, it might seem disconcertingly simple to recruit someone to a key position in a great cognac house: a

---

COGNAC

The blended cognac is returned to the casks for one to three more years, the time it takes for the different batches to fully meld. Then comes the time for bottling. And finally, impassive in its sealed bottled, the chosen cognac—whether of the finest quality and venerable age or the most modest choice of a new initiate—awaits the moment when it will breathe its last ecstatic sigh.

It was also a question of trust when, two months later, the group announced the appointment of Valérie Chapoulaud-Floquet as CEO, following the retirement of Jean-Marie Laborde. There was great astonishment in the liquor world, where people had been expecting a man from the inner circle and were presented instead with a woman from the luxury sector, whose experience ranged from L'Oréal to Louis Vuitton. Analysts were skeptical, if not outright ironic or openly critical of the choice made by the president, François Hériard Dubreuil. The previous financial year had been particularly turbulent, with the Chinese market experiencing a sharp decline due to a so-called "anti-gift" law aimed at combating ostentation and corruption. The law had a heavy impact on the cognac market, as cognac is a very popular gift in China; as a result, Rémy Martin's worldwide sales plummeted by 30 percent. The group's profits took a nosedive, so it was downgraded by financial rating agencies and relegated to high-risk borrower status. There were even rumors of a takeover. And now the triumvirate was appointing as CEO someone who had never sold a single bottle of liquor?

In fact, they were neither crazy nor reckless; they knew what they were doing. A lot of careful thought had gone into this additional step toward the world of luxury, and they had decided it would be a greater risk to continue as before, out of caution or cowardice. What the analysts and competitors said was of little importance; what mattered most was faith in the future. And the future of the group was not to be just another liquor producer, but to assert itself as the leading producer of exceptional liquors. A temporary upset, even in a major market such as China, would not divert the ship from its course. Moreover, Rémy Martin, which had increased the purchase prices it paid to the winegrowers and distillers in 2012, maintained them in 2013.

> **THE PEOPLE OF CHARENTE KNOW THAT THERE ARE GOOD YEARS AND NOT-SO-GOOD ONES; TIME ALONE CAN OVERCOME THE VAGARIES OF THE ECONOMY.**

In a world of immediacy and social media, in a financial world more interested in a company's quarterly results than in its long-term goals, in a world of growing distrust and fear of risk, Rémy Martin has a unique relationship with time. The people of Charente know that there are good years and not-so-good ones; time alone can overcome the vagaries of the economy, and can, paradoxically, even be a factor of serenity. Pierrette Trichet was well aware of this, being more concerned to meet the demand for the VSOP in four years' time than for Louis XIII some fifty or a hundred years down the line.

TASTING. Cognac is not only drunk in moderation; it is savored, slowly and with devotion. Having undergone the test of fire, it then undergoes the test of ice. Contrary to common belief, a good cognac should not be warmed by cradling the glass in one's hands: this results in the loss of the most volatile, elegant part of its fragrance. While this trick can be used to stimulate a flavorless *eau-de-vie* for a brief moment, it is wrong for a cognac. An ice cube, on the other hand, will do no harm. A powerful cognac will stand up to the cold, which in fact brings out its more subtle nuances. You can also drink cognac with soda water, as the bubbles accent the depth of its bouquet.

2015 Cinema seemed an appropriate means of expressing the special relationship between Louis XIII and the passing of time. On November 18, 2015, a project called "100 Years, The Movie You Will Never See," was undertaken in Los Angeles. It began with a simple idea: some exceptional eaux-de-vie selected in 2015 would be aged under the watchful eye of Baptiste Loiseau and his successors, to go into the blend for the Louis XIII of 2115. John Malkovich, the most Francophile American actor, was asked to write the script and play the lead role in a movie directed by Robert Rodriguez, which would not be screened until a century later. The screening is scheduled for November 18, 2115, at the Grollet Estate. A thousand tickets for this premiere have been distributed to a lucky few clients who will never see the movie, but can pass the invitations on to their descendants. Nothing more will be divulged until the screening day. The press has only been allowed to see the trailer—and even then, only after agreeing to part with their cell phones and recording devices on the day of the presentation. Since then, the mysterious reel has been locked away in a specially designed safe, to which there is no key or code, but which will open by itself when the big day comes.

> A THOUSAND TICKETS FOR THIS PREMIERE HAVE BEEN DISTRIBUTED TO A LUCKY FEW CLIENTS WHO WILL NEVER SEE THE MOVIE.

For the operation to be meaningful, the Charente terroir must still be producing cognac in 2115, although the current period is one of growing concern about climate change and, more generally, the impact of human activities on the Earth. Looking so far ahead is a motivation to amplify the sustainable development goals in all of the group's activities, beginning with the vineyards. In 2012, the 593 acres (240 hectares) of the Rémy Martin estates were the first in the Charente region to obtain an HEV (High Environmental Value) certificate, guaranteeing that their agricultural practices preserve the natural ecosystem and reduce pressure on

COGNAC

You can drink it in a cocktail, as in Hong Kong, or, in the fashion of the Dutch seamen in centuries gone by, with plain water. Before, during, or after a meal, cognac is always cognac. A tradition here, a new fashion there: it is all a revival of an old one, the "Fine à l'eau," or cognac with water, of the postwar years. Cognac is ready for anything, provided you treat it with respect.

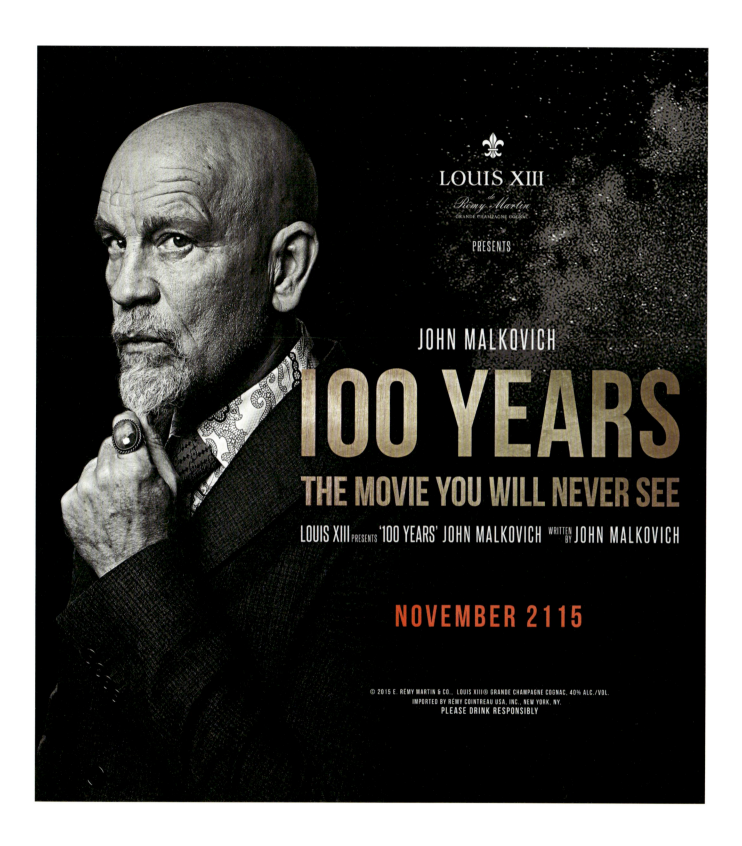

100 Years: The Movie You Will Never See; this film, shot in 2015 with John Malkovich, was locked inside a safe that will remain sealed until 2115. A countdown clock is ticking, pending the release date.

the environment to a minimum. However, this progress is only meaningful if it is widespread. In addition to the Rémy Martin estates, which provide only a fraction of the company's supply, the real challenge is to enable all the winegrowers producing for Rémy Martin to adopt the same approach. An ambitious customized training program—the first of its kind in the region—was set up, and the partner winegrowers were quick to sign up for it. By 2020, half of them were awarded the highest certification in the High Environmental Value program, and they should all be certified by 2028 or before. Christophe Forget, winegrower and president of the Alliance Fine Champagne since 2016, is passionately committed to this project, which goes far beyond simply protecting the environment. The collective approach is also a means of reconnecting with the cooperative spirit of 1966, and gives each winegrower a sense of pride at being in the service of the land.

However, everyone knows that this is just a first step. Countless avenues remain to be explored at the Juillac-le-Coq distillery and among the partner winegrowers to ensure that the Charente vineyards will continue to produce the same quality of wine in the future, for the same quality of cognac. Some growers are testing more disease-resistant grape varieties. The Monbadon grape, for example, was abandoned because it matures too late—a characteristic that is now becoming an asset.

Elsewhere, a project aims to reduce the frequency of treatments by three quarters through preventive and biological methods. Elsewhere again, a partnership between Rémy Martin and the Centre National d'Etudes Spatiales space agency is experimenting with highly precise satellite monitoring of the condition of each plot of land, with a view to more targeted and efficient interventions that will do less damage to the environment. Philippe Farnier, CEO of Rémy Martin from 2018 to 2022, was an active participant in this commitment to sustainable development from the vine to the bottle—a "Sustainable Exception" strategy, to use the expression he once suggested to the group—which will continue to develop in the future.

LOOKING SO FAR AHEAD IS A MOTIVATION TO AMPLIFY THE SUSTAINABLE DEVELOPMENT GOALS IN ALL OF THE GROUP'S ACTIVITIES, BEGINNING WITH THE VINEYARDS.

Preserving the future also means thinking about the oak from which the barrels and casks are made. Oak trees require time too. In 2010, Rémy Martin joined forces with the Office National des Forêts forestry office to carry out a series of long-term experiments on the famous Pedunculate Oak from the Limousin region, whose fairly large grain supports the specific quality of the cognac. The aim of the

Before serving a glass, take a good look at the bottle. It, too, is integral to the cognac. Pour the cognac and observe it, appreciating the intensity of its color. Before the first sip, inhale its fragrance, not once but twice; there's a hint of apricot and gingerbread, rose and dried tobacco. The Champagne crus release their floral scents, and the Limousin oak, its scent of vanilla. A very old cognac adds notes of jasmine, saffron, and sandalwood, with a hint of port wine and dried fruit.

experiments is to assess the ability of the Pedunculate Oak to adapt to climate change. However, producing the wood is one thing, and making the barrels is quite another. The traditional *tierçon* barrels that are essential for aging Louis XIII had not been made since the First World War. Each of them was pampered over the decades, repaired when necessary, and from time to time, one of the oldest *tierçons* would be sacrificed to recover a few of its staves, which were then mounted on other barrels still in working order. But the fact had to be faced: the day would come when there would not be enough *tierçons* for Louis XIII which, in the final phase of its aging process, flourishes in *tierçons* over a century old.

In the early 2010s, it was decided to relaunch the production of *tierçon* barrels. After some historical research into the principles of their construction, a stave-maker from the Limousin was called in to help. As *tierçons* are longer and more voluminous than standard barrels, he had to adapt one of his machines to split the wood to the necessary length. A first prototype was made in 2013, in partnership with the Seguin Moreau cooperage, and since 2017 some fifteen new *tierçons* have been produced each year. They are all still being matured with young eaux-de-vie. If all goes well, they will receive their first Louis XIII blends sometime in the second half of the century. When the audience of John Malkovich's movie tastes Louis XIII in 2115, it will perhaps have come from one of these barrels.

PRESERVING THE FUTURE ALSO MEANS THINKING ABOUT THE OAK FROM WHICH THE BARRELS AND CASKS ARE MADE.

The future Louis XIII cognac aging in *tierçon* barrels.

COGNAC

Before tasting, moisten your lips with a few drops of cognac to gently tease awake your taste buds. With the first sip, judge the suppleness, warmth, and mellowness of the cognac, behind the directness of the alcohol. With the second sip, discover more distant and mysterious shores, the long-lingering tastes typical of a Fine Champagne cognac. Give in to the moment, let go, eyes closed and spirit open to introspection.

Producing the *tierçon* barrels:
an enduring ancestral know-how.

2022 The company is now 300 years old, and the atmosphere is serene. Anne-Marie and André Hériard Dubreuil's children have passed it down to the next generation, with a sense of having played their part. In 2022, Marie-Amélie de Leusse became Chairwoman of the group's Board of Directors, and her cousin Caroline Bois was appointed Vice Chairwoman. Their cousin Élie Hériard Dubreuil is still present at their sides. Dominique Hériard Dubreuil doesn't visit as much, and her little Fiat 500 shows up less often in the parking lot. In 2008, she was selected by Fortune magazine as one of the world's most powerful women in business. Having devoted her heart and soul to the family business, she can now take a step back, as her father did before her. The same is true for her brothers François and Marc, who get involved only when they are needed. But there is nothing to stop them from dreaming about the future of the group, in China or Africa, or from coming up with the kind of forward-thinking idea that can blossom on the strength of wisdom and experience.

When it comes to implementing such ideas, they can turn to Éric Vallat, who became CEO of the group in 2019 after a few years at the head of the cognac house, and is now at the helm of the company and in regular contact with the Hériard Dubreuil family. Although not officially a member of the family, he relishes the pleasure of running a real family business. He had not been in office long when he had to face some challenging situations, such as the threat of tariffs on cognac imports (a hostage in the trade dispute between Europe and the United States), and the consequences of the Covid pandemic which, for the first time, forced the unprecedented closure of all the group's distilleries at the same time. But Rémy Cointreau stayed true to its course, just as it had in 2008 and 2013.

In Cognac, Jean-Philippe Hecquet was appointed CEO of Rémy Martin in 2022. He ensures the link between the historic house of Rémy Martin and the Rémy Cointreau group, with "one eye on the vines and the other on the ends of the earth," as Champaco's first chairman, Paul Hosteing, used to say.

COGNAC

Tasting is an intimate journey to private memories, to the smells of childhood, those of a grandmother's kitchen, a favorite field, the woods you used to explore. While there are those with more sensitive noses, capable of identifying a particular fleeting flavor, cognac is not reserved to an elite few. It gives generously to anyone who accepts it with sincerity and humility.

THE SPIRIT OF COGNAC

The Drop: an innovative and unique format for Louis XIII, 2022.

With the close support of the family, Hecquet has the extraordinary privilege of overseeing Rémy Martin's three-hundredth anniversary celebrations, which will inevitably recall the unforgettable festivities of 1974.

THE COMPANY IS NOW 300 YEARS OLD, AND THE ATMOSPHERE IS SERENE.

The old buildings on Rue de la Société-Vinicole have been completely renovated. There is nothing ostentatious about the place, despite its three centuries of history. It is neither a château nor a museum, but still a house—a place to meet friends and clients from the other side of the world or from the local region. There is nothing more to say: a visit to such a place cannot be described, it must be experienced, listened to, looked at, tasted, and smelled. Visitors can extend their visit at the distillery in Juillac-le-Coq, or at the family home in Le Grollet—or they can head to Merpins, where the cellars, blackened by the Torula mold, stand next to the luminous building designed by the Inca architectural firm, where the company's main services have been grouped together since 2021. The little train inaugurated in the late 1980s still does its rounds; its seats are plusher, but the magic of the visit is unchanged.

The beauty of Rémy Martin's history lies in the fact that it is a shared history, and the sincerity of that sharing is all-important. It is not the story of a brand, nor that of the two families who have taken it in turns to keep that brand alive; it is far more than that. Something reassuring and joyful underlies the three centuries of the Rémy Martin story: the idea that one can adapt to changes in the world while respecting the riches it offers. Paul-Émile Rémy Martin certainly had a dazzling intuition when he chose the centaur as the house's emblem. With his feet firmly on the earth of Charente, aiming his spear at the universe beyond, he sends a message of gratitude to those who came before, and of confidence in those who will come after.

A VISIT TO SUCH A PLACE CANNOT BE DESCRIBED, IT MUST BE EXPERIENCED, LISTENED TO, LOOKED AT, TASTED, AND SMELLED.

A great cognac, the essence of the finest wine from the finest growers, distilled in the best alembics by the best distillers, aged in the best oak casks by the best Cellar Master, is not only a remarkable collective work embodying the entire soul of a tiny corner of the world. It is a bridge between people and nature, between the earth and the sky, the past and the future. Cognac is an emotion, pure and simple. Those who have experienced it must surely pardon the angels who slip unseen into the cellars each year, for a few stolen sips from the casks.

The Rémy Martin headquarters,
Rue de la Société-Vinicole in Cognac.

PHOTOGRAPHIC CREDITS

p.6 © Robert Doisneau / Gamma Rapho - p.8 (bottom) Bibliothèque de Cognac © Aline Aubert - p.9 © Collection Maison Rémy Martin - p.10 © BNF - p.11 © Collection Maison Rémy Martin - p.11 (bottom) © Alberto Bocos Gil - p.12 (bottom) © Gérard Martron - p.13 © Collection Maison Rémy Martin - p.14 © Collection Maison Rémy Martin - p.14 (bottom) © Collection Maison Rémy Martin - p.15 © Collection Maison Rémy Martin - p.16 © Collection Maison Rémy Martin - p.16 (bottom) © Stéphane Charbeau - p.17 © Collection Maison Rémy Martin - p.18 © Collection Maison Rémy Martin - p.18 (bottom) © Yann Arthus-Bertrand - p.19 © Collection Maison Rémy Martin. - p.20 © Collection Maison Rémy Martin - p.21 © Collection Maison Rémy Martin - p.21 (bottom) © Alberto Bocos Gil - p.22 © Collection Maison Rémy Martin - p.22 (bottom) © Alberto Bocos Gil - p.23 © Patrick Bertrand / Rémy Martin - p.24 © Collection Maison Rémy Martin - p.24 (bottom) © Stéphane Charbeau - p.25 © Collection Maison Rémy Martin - p.26 © Collection Maison Rémy Martin - p.27 (bottom) © Worcester Art Museum / Museum purchase / Bridgeman Images - p.28 © Société nationale d'Horticulture de France - p.28 (bottom) © Bridgeman Images - p.29 © Collection Maison Rémy Martin - p.30–31 © Collection Maison Rémy Martin - p.32 © Collection Maison Rémy Martin - p.33 © Henry Billard - p.33 (bottom) © British Library Board. All Rights Reserved / Bridgeman Images - p.34 © Collection Maison Rémy Martin - p.34 © Collection Maison Rémy Martin - p.34 (bottom) © Index Fototeca / Bridgeman Images - p.35 All Rights Reserved - p.36 © Collection Maison Rémy Martin - p.36 (bottom) © Jules Troncy / Collection Maison Rémy Martin - p.37 (top) © Henry Billard - p.37 (bottom) © Henry Billard - p.38 © Collection Maison Rémy Martin - p.38 (bottom) © Alberto Bocos Gil - p.39 (top) © Collection Maison Rémy Martin - p.39 (bottom) All Rights Reserved - p.40–41 © Harry Gruyaert / Magnum Photos - p.42–43 © Harry Gruyaert / Magnum Photos - p.44–45 © Harry Gruyaert / Magnum Photos - p.46 © Jacques Goguet / Rémy Martin - p.48 © Collection Maison Rémy Martin - p.48 (bottom) © Alberto Bocos Gil - p.49 All Rights Reserved - p.50 © Jacques Goguet / Rémy Martin - p.51 (bottom) © Patrick Bertrand / Rémy Martin - p.52 © Roger-Viollet / Roger-Viollet - p.52 (bottom) © Alberto Bocos Gil - p.53 © Collection Maison Rémy Martin - p.54 © Jacques Goguet / Rémy Martin - p.54 (bottom) © Alberto Bocos Gil - p.56 (left) © Collection Maison Rémy Martin - p.56 (right) © Collection Maison Rémy Martin - p.56 (bottom) © Alberto Bocos Gil - p.57 © Jacques Goguet / Rémy Martin - p.58 (bottom) © Robert Doisneau / Gamma Rapho - p.59 © Collection Maison Rémy Martin - p.60 (bottom) © Robert Doisneau / Gamma Rapho - p.61 © Jacques Goguet / Rémy Martin - p.62 © Collection Rémy Martin - p.63 © Jacques Goguet / Rémy Martin - p.63 (bottom) © Alberto Bocos Gil - p.64–65 © Jacques Goguet / Rémy Martin - p.66 (bottom) © Harry Gruyaert / Magnum Photos - p.67 © Jacques Goguet / Rémy Martin - p.68 © Jacques Goguet / Rémy Martin - p.68 (bottom) © Robert Doisneau / Gamma Rapho - p.69 © Collection Maison Rémy Martin - p.70 © Collection Maison Rémy Martin - p.70 (bottom) © Alberto Bocos Gil - p.71 All Rights Reserved - p.72–73 © Collection Maison Rémy Martin - p.74 © Jacques Goguet / Rémy Martin - p.75 (bottom) © Alberto Bocos Gil - p.76 All Rights Reserved - p.76 (bottom) © Robert Doisneau / Gamma Rapho - p.77 © LAPI / Roger-Viollet - p.78 © Collection Rémy Martin - p.79 (bottom) © Alberto Bocos Gil - p.80 (bottom) © Erica Lansner - p.81 (top) © Jacques Goguet / Rémy Martin - p.81 (bottom) © Jacques Goguet / Rémy Martin - p.82 (top) © Robert Doisneau / Gamma Rapho - p.82 (bottom) © Robert Doisneau / Gamma Rapho - p.83 © Collection Maison Rémy Martin - p.83 (bottom) © Harry Gruyaert / Magnum Photos - p.84 © Collection Maison Rémy Martin - p.84 (bottom) © Alberto Bocos Gil - p.85 © Collection Maison Rémy Martin - p.86 (left) © Robert Doisneau / Gamma Rapho - p.86 (right) © Robert Doisneau / Gamma Rapho - p.86 (bottom) © Alberto Bocos Gil - p.87 © Robert Doisneau / Gamma Rapho - p.88–89 © Harry Gruyaert / Magnum Photos - p.90–91 © Harry Gruyaert / Magnum Photos - p.92–93 © Harry Gruyaert / Magnum Photos - p.94 © Collection Maison Rémy Martin - p.96 (bottom) © Look and Learn / Bridgeman Images - p.97 © Alberto Bocos Gil - p.98 (bottom) © Look and Learn / Bridgeman Images - p.99 © Jacques Goguet / Rémy Martin - p.100 (bottom) © British Library Board. All Rights Reserved / Bridgeman Images - p.101 All Rights Reserved - p.102 © Patrick Bertrand / Rémy Martin - p.103 (bottom) © The Holbarn Archive / Bridgeman Images - p.104 © Yvonnick Ragueneau - p.104 (bottom) © Bridgeman Images - p.105 © Denys Vinson - p.106–107 © Stéphane Charbeau - p.108 © Marc Riboud - p.108 (bottom) © The Holbarn Archive / Bridgeman Images - p.109 © Marc Riboud - p.110 © Collection Maison Rémy Martin - p.111 © Collection Maison Rémy Martin - p.111 (bottom) © North Wind Pictures / Bridgeman Images - p.112 © Collection Maison Rémy Martin - p.113 © Jacques Goguet / Rémy Martin - p.113 (bottom) © Mary Evans / Bridgeman Images - p.114 © Jean Jacques Gilbert - p.114 (bottom) © Archives Charmet / Bridgeman Images - p.115 (top) © Jacques Goguet / Rémy Martin - p.115 (bottom) © Jacques Goguet / Rémy Martin - p.116 (bottom) © Centre Historique des Archives Nationales / © Archives Charmet / Bridgeman Images - p.117 (left) © Collection Maison Rémy Martin - p.117 (right) © Collection Maison Rémy Martin - p.119 © A. Muriot ; All Rights Reserved - p.119 (bottom) © Akg / Science Photo Library - p.120 © Collection Maison Rémy Martin - p.121 © A. Muriot ; All Rights Reserved - p.121 (bottom) © Denys Vinson - p.122 © Denys Vinson - p.123 © Harry Gruyaert / Magnum Photos - p.124 © Stéphane Charbeau - p.125 © Stéphane Charbeau - p.126 (bottom) © Harry Gruyaert / Magnum Photos - p.127 © Collection Maison Rémy Martin - p.128 © Stéphane Charbeau - p.129 © Erica Lansner - p.130 (bottom) © Stéphane Charbeau - p.131 © Alberto Bocos Gil - p.132 (bottom) © Stéphane Charbeau - p.133 © Ogilvy et Mather / Rémy Martin - p.134 (bottom) © Stéphane Charbeau - p.135 © Collection Maison Rémy Martin - p.136 © Marc Riboud - p.137 (bottom) © Stéphane Charbeau - p.138 All Rights Reserved - p.139 © Collection Maison Rémy Martin - p.140 (bottom) © Marc Riboud - p.141 (top) © Yann Arthus-Bertrand - p.141 (bottom) © Patrick Bertrand / Rémy Martin - p.142–143 © Harry Gruyaert / Magnum Photos - p.144–145 © Harry Gruyaert

/ Magnum Photos - p.146–147 © Harry Gruyaert / Magnum Photos - p.148 © Dan Forbes - p.150 © Stéphane Charbeau - p.150 (bottom) © Stéphane Charbeau - p.151 © Collection Maison Rémy Martin - p.152 © Harry Gruyaert / Magnum Photos - p.153 © Patrick Bertrand / Rémy Martin - p.154 © Harry Gruyaert / Magnum Photos - p.155 © Camille Moirenc - p.156 © Pol Baril - p.156 (bottom) © Alberto Bocos Gil - p.157 © Collection Maison Rémy Martin - p.158 (left) © Collection Maison Rémy Martin - p.158 (right) © Collection Maison Rémy Martin - p.159 © Collection Maison Rémy Martin - p.159 (bottom) © GUY Christian / hemis.fr - p.160 (bottom) © Harry Gruyaert / Magnum Photos - p.161 © Aline Aubert - p.162 © Stéphane Charbeau - p.163 (top, left) © Partizan / Rémy Martin - p.163 © James Bort - p.164 (bottom) © Stéphane Charbeau - p.165 © Artcurial SAS / Rémy Martin - p.166 © Collection Maison Rémy Martin - p.166 (bottom) © Aline Aubert - p.167 © Collection Maison Rémy Martin - p.168 © Collection Maison Rémy Martin - p.169 © Collection Maison Rémy Martin - p.169 (bottom) © Stéphane Charbeau - p.170 © Jean-François Ballé / We Are Social / Rémy Martin - p.171 (bottom) © Harry Gruyaert / Magnum Photos - p.172 (bottom) © Harry Gruyaert / Magnum Photos - p.173 © Benjamin Colombel - p.174 © H.F. Davis / Hulton Archive / Getty Images - p.174 (bottom) © Alberto Bocos Gil - p.175 © Tomaso Sartori - p.176 All Rights Reserved - p.176 (bottom) © Pol Baril - p.177 © James Bort - p.178 © Agence Carré Basset / Rémy Martin - p.179 (bottom) © Harry Gruyaert / Magnum Photos - p.180 © Harry Gruyaert / Magnum Photos - p.180 (bottom) © Robert Doisneau / Gamma Rapho - p.181 © Benjamin Colombel - p.182 © Bompass / Rémy Martin - p.183 © Alberto Bocos Gil - p.183 (bottom) © Robert Doisneau / Gamma Rapho - p.184 (bottom) © Harry Gruyaert / Magnum Photos - p.185 © Alberto Bocos Gil - p.186 © Julie Durand / Omedia / Rémy Martin - p.186 (bottom) © By Eve Livesey / Getty Images - p.187 © Martin Dejoie / Les Éditions d'Autils - p.188 © Alberto Bocos Gil - p.189 (bottom) © Camille Moirenc - p.190 © Aline Aubert - p.190 (bottom) © Mad Agency / Rémy Martin - p.191 © Fred & Farid / Rémy Martin - p.192 (bottom) © Anthony Costifas - p.193 © Alberto Bocos Gil - p.194 © Ramak Fazel - p.194 (top) © Aline Aubert - p.195 (top) © Pol Baril - p.195 (bottom) © Piotr Stokloza - p.196 © Yann Arthus-Bertrand - p.196 (bottom) © Didier Delmas - p.197 © Charlotte Navio / TBWA / Rémy Martin - p.198 © Franck Brouillet - p.198 (bottom) © Anthony Costifas - p.199 © Stéphane Charbeau - p.200–201 © Harry Gruyaert / Magnum Photos - p.202–203 © Harry Gruyaert / Magnum Photos - p.204–205 © Harry Gruyaert / Magnum Photos - Cover © Alberto Bocos Gil.

Despite our best efforts, we have been unable to trace the copyright owners of some of the photographs and illustrations in this book. We offer our sincere apologies, and would be pleased to insert the appropriate acknowledgments in any future editions.

Thanks to Henry Elwing.

Maison Rémy Martin
Editorial and Iconographic Direction
Florence Puech, Micaëlle Amoussou-Coussy, Camille Castanié

Éditions Flammarion
Director of Editorial Partnerships
Henri Julien

Project Manager
Mathilde Jouret

Editor
Virginie Maubourguet
assisted by Marion Cipriani

Design and Typesetting
Justeciel

Translation from the French
Lisa Davidson, Sally Laruelle

Copyediting
Kate Tombeur

Production
Corinne Trovarelli

Color Separation
Arciel Graphic

Printed in Italy by Musumeci

Simultaneously published
in French as *L'Esprit du cognac*
© Éditions Flammarion, S.A.,
Paris, 2023

English-language edition
© Éditions Flammarion, S.A.,
Paris, 2023

All rights reserved.
No part of this publication may
be reproduced in any form or by
any means, electronic, photocopy,
information retrieval system,
or otherwise, without written
permission from
Éditions Flammarion, S.A.
82 Rue Saint-Lazare
CS 10124
75009 Paris

editions.flammarion.com
@flammarioninternational

Printed in Italy by Musumeci in July 2023

THE FINE ART
of
COGNAC TASTING

BAPTISTE LOISEAU

CELLAR MASTER
FOR THE HOUSE OF RÉMY MARTIN

Tasting cognac is an experience that draws on all the senses. Sight, smell, and taste all come together in a moment of great intensity, because if you wish to capture the manifold notes that appear, disappear, and combine with one another, you must be focused. The result of age-old craftsmanship, cognac is a multi-faceted eau-de-vie.

It is also a playful partner; when mixed or blended with other ingredients, it transforms and adds that extra *je ne sais quoi* to a cocktail. With these recipes, we want to introduce you to this little-known world. They are not meant to be strict instructions to follow to the letter; quite the contrary, we encourage you to make them your own, try other combinations, and experiment with new possibilities.

Let your creativity roam free!

THE MAIN STEPS IN A TASTING

Sight

It all begins with observation. Hold your glass by its base and examine it in the light. The cognac should be gleaming and transparent. The color can vary from pale gold to dark amber. The color is determined by the oak barrels in which the cognacs are aged, not merely the length of the aging process.

The nose

Before sipping the cognac, it is important to take time to savor the aromas rising from the glass. Bring it slowly to your nose at just the right distance for appreciating all the subtleties of this nectar. Above all, don't shake it or the fragile, volatile aromas could be released too quickly. Inhale deeply. You will then perceive the fruity, floral, spicy, and even woody notes.

The palate

Cognac is tasted in small sips. Swish the first one in your mouth, so that it coats the palate. The second sip involves "chewing" the cognac to release its aromas. Take a bit more time with this step. Once you've swallowed this sip, place your tongue on your palate to detect even more aromas.

What you feel

The experience is unique and will differ depending on the type of cognac tasted and on everything that precedes the tasting.

Let's start with the first perceptions and the light notes of peach and apricot. These are followed by those of vanilla, primarily deriving from the barrel, creating a perfect harmony of fruity and woody notes. A sensation of sweetness emerges with the second sip, underscored by the aromas of fruit. And finally, for our best-quality cognacs, there will be woody aromas of mushroom and spices that impart a signature depth to cognac. The journey sometimes ends with the persistent scent of wax and walnut, which can linger in the mouth.

Four tips for correct tasting

Use a "cellar master" or tulip glass.

Pour the cognac 10 to 15 minutes prior to tasting.

Serve it at room temperature,
between 64°F and 68°F (18°C and 20°C).

Take your time.

To discover other facets of this eau-de-vie, treat yourself
to a Rémy Martin XO over ice, in a tumbler.

TIPS
FOR A GREAT COCKTAIL

1
THE RIGHT TIME

There is a cocktail for every situation and every mood. The Rémy Ginger and Centaur, for example (recipe page 8), is good for entertaining and perfect on a dance floor. The XO Old Fashioned (recipe page 9), is ideal for a more intimate moment, after dinner. Of course, this advice can (and should!) be tossed out at the drop of a hat.

2
THE RIGHT GLASS

You would never drink champagne in a whisky glass. It's the same for cocktails. The choice of a glass contributes to the visual pleasure and adds elegance to the tasting experience. The heft of the glass is also important, as it carries the drink to your mouth. Its weight and finesse certainly influence the moment.

3
THE RIGHT ICE

Similarly, ice plays a crucial role. It determines the correct dilution of the cocktail but also its temperature, which is essential for the taste. Choose an ice cube size that is adapted to the drink, preferably ice that has been frozen at -4°F (-20°C) as it melts more slowly. For purists, "clear ice" is frozen in motion to prevent the formation of air bubbles. It is denser than regular ice.

4
THE RIGHT PROPORTIONS

As with baking, making a good cocktail is all about the correct measurements. And for that, you'll need a jigger, an inverted measuring cup. Once you have mastered the proportions, you can move past them and give free rein to your creativity.

5
THE RIGHT INGREDIENTS —
AND HEART!

As in the kitchen, use local and seasonal ingredients as much as possible. And put your heart and intention into it, because in mixology, it is, of course, all about sharing.

Three ways to make a cocktail

The Shaker
All the ingredients, including the ice, are mixed together in a shaker, then poured into the cocktail glass.

The Build Method
The cocktail is prepared directly in the glass in which it will be served; a gentle stir with a bar spoon gives it all its flavour.

Blended
All the ingredients are mixed in a glass, then served in another glass, which increases the degree of dilution.

LEGENDARY COCKTAILS

These classics never go out of style

Rémy Ginger or Centaur

Inspired by the Horse's Neck, this iconic drink is the ideal starting point for exploring the world of cocktails. A cool, spicy long drink, it is easy to make at home. Perfectly balanced, it showcases the famous Rémy Martin VSOP's aromatic notes.

HISTORY
It gets its name from the twist of lemon peel curling up and over the top of the glass, like the curve of a horse's neck.

OCCASION
A festive afternoon cocktail that's great even on the dance floor. Light and refreshing, it's definitely a drink to share with others.

RECIPE
Rémy Martin VSOP (5 cl) / Angostura bitters (3 dashes) / Ginger ale (10 cl) / A long twist of lemon peel

GLASS
Long drink, tumbler

METHOD
Build

Sidecar

To describe this cocktail, let's look to American spirits expert Paul Pacult: "The Sidecar has a good acidity upfront that promotes a crisp, citrusy flavor profile. It has a dry, astringent finish, fruity and spicy, rich and tart at the same time."

HISTORY
The Sidecar is thought to have been invented in 1921, then imported to France. According to tradition, the Ritz in Paris first served a premium version of the cocktail in 1923, mixed with a Rémy Martin cognac that predated phylloxera, the pest that destroyed French vineyards in the nineteenth century. The rarity of this eau-de-vie made this the most expensive cocktail in the world.

OCCASION
As an aperitif, in a hotel bar, of course. It's a strong cocktail, to savor slowly.

RECIPE
Rémy Martin 1738 Accord Royal (3 cl) / Cointreau (2 cl) / Lemon juice (1 cl)

GLASS
Martini glass or small coupe glass

METHOD
Shaker

XO Old Fashioned

If we were talking about music, this would be the soloist, as it showcases Rémy Martin XO. It is also one of the only cocktails that requires you to wait a few minutes for the ice to dissolve to fully appreciate its flavor.

HISTORY
Some say the Old Fashioned originated in New Orleans and was created in the 1840s, during the golden age of brown spirits.

OCCASION
For dessert, enjoy with a fruit tart, or sitting in front of a fireplace with a cat curled up on your lap.

RECIPE
Rémy Martin XO (5 cl) / 1 cube of brown sugar / Angostura bitters (3 dashes)

GLASS
Old Fashioned

METHOD
Blended

SIGNATURE COCKTAILS

These recipes were created by Cédric Bouteiller, mixologist for the house of Rémy Martin

Alliance

A floral, fairly sweet cocktail,
with exotic notes conjuring faraway places.

HISTORY

This cocktail was created for the first Rencontres Fine Champagne, held in 2021, a major annual event for Rémy Martin that celebrates the eight hundred winegrower members of the Alliance Fine Champagne cooperative.

OCCASION

Late afternoon or early evening, after leaving a meeting for a drink together. Great for a group of friends.

RECIPE

Rémy Martin VSOP (4.5 cl) / Extra-dry vermouth (1 cl) / Elderflower syrup (1 cl) / verjuice (1 cl) / Cold-brewed Cape Town rooibos tea (7 cl)

GLASS

Long drink, tumbler

METHOD

Build

Harmony

A tart, ambrosial cocktail. It's a crowd-pleaser,
combining the flavors of orgeat syrup and apple juice—
a genuine Proustian drink, inspired by local ingredients.

HISTORY

Created for the 2017 Congrès des Œnologues, this cocktail is fast becoming timeless.

OCCASION

A slightly tart, fruity cocktail to share while entertaining, ideal for discovering the scope of cognac's aromatic palette.

RECIPE

Rémy Martin VSOP (5 cl) / Orgeat syrup (0.5 cl) / Verjuice (1 cl) / Fresh apple juice (7 cl)

GLASS

Long drink

METHOD

Build

INSPIRED COCKTAILS

Dazzling recipes to dream big

Fleurissimo

A fruity, sparkling cocktail
with a touch of acidity.

HISTORY

This cocktail is a tribute to Grace Kelly, a princess who loved floral fragrances and the atmosphere of hotel bars. It was created by Agostino Perrone, director of mixology at the Connaught Hotel in London, home to one of the world's best bars.

OCCASION

For an aperitif, in a chic and cozy hotel bar.

RECIPE

Rémy Martin VSOP (1.5 cl) / Crème de violette (0.5 cl) / 1 sugar cube / top with champagne

GLASS

Nick & Nora glass

METHOD

Build

Paragon of Grit

An exceptional cocktail combining
equally exceptional ingredients.

HISTORY

This surprising cocktail earned its creator, Josephine Sanglo from Sweden, first prize at the 2019 Bartender Talent Academy. This annual international competition in Cognac brings together the world's best mixologists.

OCCASION

At the end of the day, a cocktail for an introspective moment.

RECIPE

Rémy Martin XO (4.5 cl) / Rhubarb vermouth (3 cl) / Hōjicha tea syrup (1 cl) / Absinthe (2 drops) / Angostura bitters (2 drops)

GLASS

Small coupe glass

METHOD

Blend

PAIRING WITH FOOD

Pairing is not easy to do. It requires inspiration and exploration—and tasting several blends to find the perfect combination. But what makes a good pairing?

A good pairing is one that creates contrast or a complementary flavor. The contrast may come from the texture, between crispy and soft for example, but also from the taste, with a combination of acid and sweet flavors. A complementary approach means detecting similar notes in each of the ingredients that create a harmony, for example, a smoky dish with a drink that has woody aromas. Other pairings can reveal different facets in a way that makes one plus one equal five—where the whole is much greater than the individual parts. This is how you can draw on what you already know to dream up your own pairings, because what really matters with cocktails is to having fun.

RÉMY MARTIN VSOP TASTING NOTES
Dried apricot, licorice, summer fruits like peach,
candied pear, vanilla.

A MENU PAIRED FROM START TO FINISH

Appetizer
Rémy Martin VSOP on ice (in a glass pre-cooled with an ice cube) and oysters.
Why does it work?
The briny flavor of the oysters brings out the sweet aromas of Rémy Martin VSOP.

Main course
Rémy Martin VSOP served iced, from a freezer (-18°C) with raw fish,
for example salmon sashimi served with a touch of wasabi.
Why does it work?
The textured flavors contrast with the cold cognac, creating a balance that brings out the tension between the sweetness and the acidity, and on the finish,
a crisp sensation that explodes on the palate.

Cheese
Rémy Martin VSOP served neat with Roquefort.
Why does it work?
Roquefort's buttery and salty notes bring out cognac's dried fruit aromas.
In terms of texture, the pairing also works between the creamy aspect of
the cheese and the freshness of the cognac.

Dessert
Rémy Martin VSOP served neat with a vanilla macaron.
Why does it work?
The vanilla notes in the macaron harmoniously echo those of the cognac.

A pairing that doesn't work well (for now)
Rémy Martin VSOP with truffles.
Why not?
The powerful truffle notes tend to overwhelm
those of Rémy Martin VSOP.

RÉMY MARTIN VSOP TASTING NOTES
Plum, candied orange, passion fruit, hazelnut, nutmeg, roasted cocoa bean, honey, jasmine, ginger, saffron, walnut, gingerbread.

A MENU PAIRED FROM START TO FINISH

Appetizer
Rémy Martin XO on ice with foie gras.
Why does it work?
The foie gras brings out the woody aromas of the Rémy Martin XO, which derive primarily from the barrel in which it was aged.

Main course
Rémy Martin XO with Beef Wellington, a fillet of beef coated with mushrooms and hazelnuts and wrapped in puff pastry.
Why does it work?
The meaty aspect of the dish echoes the woody aromas of Rémy Martin XO cognac, two notes in the same chord, creating a delicious pairing.

Cheese
Rémy Martin XO with Parmesan.
Why does it work?
Parmesan is rich in umami, one of the five basic tastes primarily present in proteins. That's why it pairs so beautifully with the delicate flavors of Rémy Martin XO.

Dessert
Rémy Martin XO, chilled to 41°F (5°C) in the refrigerator, with a chocolate fondant.
Why does it work?
The deep chocolate notes reveal the complexity of the cognac aromas, for a lovely, introspective moment.

A pairing that doesn't work well (for now)
Rémy Martin XO and tabasco.
Why not?
While the spiciness of certain ingredients, such as ginger, pair perfectly with Rémy Martin XO cognac, this combination no longer works when one of them scorches the taste buds.

Texts
MATHILDE FENESTRAZ

Illustrations
JULIA PERRIN

PLEASE DRINK RESPONSIBLY